PATH

Praise for *Path*

"This simple story brought me to a beautiful place. And then it showed me how to live there."

—Mel Bermudes

"*Path* is a beautiful journey of self-discovery.
A much-needed guide to walking the path of life responsibly, lovingly and creatively. Filled with sweet moments
of recognition and sighs of relief, it provides practical
tools for living a healthy and inspired life."

**—Joel Altman,
founder, Hariharalaya Meditation
Retreat Centre**

"*Path* really reminded me and hooked me like *The Alchemist* or any Paulo Coelho book. Those are the only books
I sit and read cover to cover in one sitting."

—Hugo Byron

"This book is a conversation that I felt like I should be having with someone else only to realize I needed to be having it with myself. I have needed this book for the last twelve years of my life. As an educator, I love the philosophy and new knowledge I gained. As a human, I fell in love with the characters and the story. I want my colleagues and students to read this book."

—Gerson Castro, high school teacher, San Jose

"This book meant so much to me personally. It has come along at exactly the right time. I feel like a good friend would say, 'Read this. Read this now.'"

— Lucy Carmody

"The framework and themes—and the advice—are thoughtful and intelligent and provocative. At forty-seven, with a bit of life behind me, I relate to the choices and the minds, the winding path, the holes we learn to walk around."

—Julian Hirst

PATH

A Story of Love, a Guide to Life

J.E. CHADWICK

TURF
TAVERN
PRESS

Oxford – Palo Alto – Singapore

Copyright © 2020 by J. E. Chadwick

First paperback edition April 2020

Cover art © 2020 by Coverkitchen
Interior design & typesetting by Coverkitchen
Interior illustrations by Lawrence Perry

ISBN 978-1-7347445-0-7 (paperback)
ISBN 978-1-7347445-1-4 (ebook)

Printed and bound in United States of America
First printing April 2020

www.jechadwick.com

To my family
&
my forever friends.

And to all who feel
this book was written just for them.

It was.

Contents

Preface

Dear children, nieces and nephews,

I wrote this book for you.

It's a message in a bottle sent to a shipwrecked future version of you.

Some of you helped me to write and illustrate it, but I doubt if any of you will understand it until the day you need it.

Perhaps that day is today. Maybe this is the first morning you saw a stranger in the mirror, and you've decided to find out who you really are.

If this is that day, then *Path* should help you face it down.

The boy in this story is me in all of his restless vanity. When I was a teenager, I became sick and imagined a hundred reasons not to live. I believed there was only one right path, and it was blocked. Then one day I walked out alone and discovered many new roads. Eventually, I came home happy and strong again.

The girl in this story is every friend and teacher I ever had. I hope you fall in love with her. If you ever meet someone like her, never let them go.

The guide to a good life is real. It took me thirty years to learn it the hard way. The next time you hit a wall or fall into a hole, try it for a week or two. If it works, stick with it.

I call it PATH: a *practical aid to happiness*. It's a simple guide to understand, but you will still need to put in the effort to walk it, if you choose to.

I wrote a story because I didn't know how else to tell you everything in it.

I kept it short so you could finish it in a day.

I wrote about love because a life without love isn't worth the effort required to live it.

They say that by the time a man realizes his father was sometimes right, he has sons of his own who think he's always wrong. If you live a full life, perhaps one day you'll write a book for your own children to ignore on a dusty shelf.

Until then, take every path you can, and I will be with you.

Your father, your uncle, and your friend forever,

JEC, March 2020

The End

A boy placed his palms onto the cold steel railing and leaned out. He pushed up onto his toes and hauled himself up. Flakes of red paint dug into his soft fingers as he peered far down through the night fog at the icy water. He wiped his salty nostrils on his sleeve and shuddered, wondering about the impact.

They call it the coward's way out, he thought, but it didn't feel cowardly. It would be like hitting pavement, shattering his spine and ripping his guts open into the black waters of the strait. Shark food for the Golden Gate. Only two in every hundred jumpers survive.

He shuddered again. He'd never thought about ending his life before this week. But here he was alone on that bridge for the third night in a row.

It was enough. It was time.

The unraveling had begun a few months earlier.

He sat in a cold hospital room while his father was dying of cancer. He sat and watched the quiet terror in his eyes.

"Let me know what you need me to do," the boy asked, quite unprepared to do anything.

He had arrived overnight on the red-eye, summoned by a one-line message from his mother: "You should come now to see your dad."

He had sensed that something was wrong for a while, but they'd told him nothing. Now he was unprepared for the acrid smell of the hospital ward and the sight of his father's matchstick limbs and hollow gaze.

His father was unable to smile at him. "Be a good boy," he rasped.

"I will, Dad. I promise I will."

The boy wept quietly as his thoughts screamed.

What exactly does good mean to you, Dad?

Am I still a boy to you? Am I not a man now?

What have you learned in sixty years?

Why didn't you call for me earlier?

"I will look after Mom," he whispered. "I promise." He reached under the plastic tubes for the limp grey hand that lay on the bed. "Dad, is there anything you want to tell me? About...anything? About life?"

Silent eyes, a coughing fit, and then a few last words.

"You'll work it out. Be a good boy." And finally: "I don't like this anymore."

Is this really how people die? This inarticulate darkness?

The funeral was a quiet affair with a dozen friends and neighbors. The boy wore his father's musty black suit. A handwritten eulogy was curled up in the jacket pocket. His mother had asked him not to deliver it. She'd said it wasn't that kind of service.

The next morning, after breakfast, his mother took his hands in hers and told him to fly back to San Francisco.

"Your dad arranged everything long ago, so you don't need to worry about me. There's money for both of us." She still hadn't cried. "I don't need you here now, and I want to be alone in the house. Come back for Thanksgiving perhaps, if you want to."

He told her he wanted to stay and look after her for a while, but she insisted on being alone. He called to change his flight and then went up to his room to pack.

He sat there on his old bunk bed and wept as the memories of his childhood home flooded in. The crunch of his father's hands rummaging through boxes of Lego. The stain on the carpet from a chemistry set he'd received on his eleventh birthday. Marks on the wall where dozens of his drawings had once hung—several experiments in style, none quite encouraged.

He looked over at the small pine desk. Most of all he recalled the thousands of lamplit hours he spent working anxiously to get the grades he needed to earn offers of admission to the colleges on his parents' list. When the offers arrived, they enjoyed a celebratory meal at Il Forno.

"You worked hard for this." His father waved the letter from Stanford in the air. "And it will all pay off when you get to California." He smiled proudly at him over his pasta.

But did it pay off, Dad?

He flew back west the next day, lightheaded and desperate to get back to Claudia at their apartment. She was the only person who understood him. They'd met in the city while he was volunteering at the dog rescue shelter in his first week after graduation. They bonded over a bundle of puppies, followed by fish tacos, margaritas, and laughter. Even his roommate and business partner Jonah approved of her.

"Man, she's way out of your league!" Jonah had confirmed. She moved in a week later.

Now he needed her so much it hurt. Especially the night he flew back.

"I can't even imagine what it was like." She held him tight before he could get through the doorway. "You should have let me come with you."

"It was awful." He fought back his tears. "I can't believe he's gone already. I never even knew who he was. He had nothing to say, no words for me."

"Oh, baby, I'm so sorry. Come to bed. It's going to be OK." But it wasn't.

They didn't argue for the first few weeks. They kept busy with their jobs and the shelter. They ate out every night and avoided their friends. The news headlines warned of a disturbing new virus exploding across Asia and Europe, and there were already a dozen cases reported across the city. People were scared, and most of the usual events were getting canceled, which suited him fine.

He had bad days, and he had worse days. His mood often turned dark. She hated his aggressive tone whenever he talked to her and the long silences when he didn't.

"I know you're hurting," she said one night, "but I'm not the enemy here. Not every conversation needs to be an argument. I'm not somebody you have to beat in a debate. I already know you're smart. I also need to know you care."

He shook his head in disbelief, but she continued.

"You need to climb out of this. You're all knotted up and turning in on yourself. Try to spend more time with your friends."

"I'm sorry I don't have a happy button I can just switch on. I'm going through a process to get through this. I'll get back to one hundred percent normal. I'll hang out with everyone when I'm finished and I'm ready."

He told her he needed more time. She said she could wait, but she wasn't sure why she had to.

Then, on one foggy morning, he left for work but returned five minutes later for his jacket, only to find Jonah and Claudia already singing in the shower together.

What the…?

They didn't try to lie to him. It wasn't the first time, they said. It was a big relief that he knew about it now, they told him.

"Well, it's not a relief *for me!*" he screamed.

It would be better if he moved out.

His life unraveled fast from that point.

Jonah soon began to oust him from the startup they had founded together and sued him for negligence. Their investors stopped returning his calls. A few friends sent him messages but never more than one. The first few virus cases in his neighborhood had been reported, and the streets were starting to empty, apart from anxious shoppers stockpiling food and giant packs of toilet paper. He found a room in a quiet apartment nearby and raged, pinballing between anger, shame, and emptiness. He started walking the city at night with the other insomniacs, and he eventually found the bridge.

There he was, alone in the fog for the third night, gripping cold steel.

It was enough.

It was time.

But something wasn't right. This wasn't the right place.

It might be the world's favorite place to die, but it wasn't calling his name. He hated this city now with all of his heart. It had betrayed him, and he didn't want to die in it.

But if not here, then where?

He'd always liked the mountains more than the city. What if he were to fall while climbing an impossible rock face? Free solo. No ropes, no harnesses. Just him on a silent mountain, pushing up as high as he could until he fell.

Yes, there.

He returned home, grabbed his camping gear, and ran through the foggy streets to the bus station. He boarded the first Greyhound bus headed to the mountains, and he slept for the first time in a week.

When he awoke, he could see only lakes and trees through the bus window. At the next stop, he stepped off so he could hitch a ride higher up into the mountains.

The Crossroads

A rusty red Chevy pulled up beside a sequoia grove, and the boy jumped down. He yanked his backpack from the flatbed and gave a short wave to the driver as the truck rattled away.

He took a moment to breathe in the Sierra Nevada air, then stepped toward the grove's dark entrance and peered in. Shafts of dusty sunlight lit up the path, inviting him through the trees, and he set off uphill at a brisk pace. Eyes down, shallow breaths, tight lips.

After an hour, the ground started to level off, and the boy could see a break in the trees ahead. He stepped out into a wide mountain meadow. Countless shades of green sprinkled with flowers—and, above, an electric-blue sky. A stream snaked down the middle of the valley from as far as the stern mountains beyond.

Yes, here.

A tiny hummingbird startled him, its shimmering body upright as it fell out of nowhere and hovered just above his forehead. The buzz of its wings throbbed in his ears as they faced each other for a moment, eye to eye. Then, like an acrobat, the bird twisted backward and dropped down to sip nectar from a flame-red wildflower in the long grass.

Yes, here.

The scene took his breath away, and he allowed himself a rare smile. He swigged icy water from his flask. He would walk to the giant rock face and climb at night. It might take a day or two to reach it, he couldn't tell, and he could pitch his tent along the way. But first he needed to figure out how to get there. He stood at a crossroads where several dirt paths converged, and it wasn't clear which one he should take.

"How hard would it be to put up a signpost?" he asked aloud in frustration.

"Does everything in life need a signpost?" came a girl's voice from behind him.

The boy, surprised, attempted to spin around but tumbled backward, dropping his water flask. The girl laughed. She was crouched upon a giant boulder, looking down at him. His face burned red. She must have been watching him the whole time.

"I'm sorry," he said. "I had no idea you were up there. I thought I was alone. Was I talking to myself?"

The girl laughed again. "Don't apologize! We all talk to ourselves, always. It's everybody's dirty little secret. If you ever transcribed the ramblings of your mind, it would read like the ravings of a madman. Yet few people ever sit still enough to listen to their own voice."

She could have been his age or a dozen years older; it was impossible to tell. She spoke confidently with a slight accent, something European or perhaps Québécois. She smiled at him with fine, dark features.

"Well," he said, "It's hardly madness to ask for a signpost at a crossroads. Is it? I just need to choose one of these paths, but without a signpost I'm kinda guessing."

"Perhaps. If you believe some paths are wrong and some

are right, then I can see why you might want a sign. But not if you believe all paths are unknowable and have an equal chance of leading you to a good place. Perhaps then a signpost would just confuse you or make you anxious."

He looked up at the girl and wondered how the conversation had gotten so philosophical. He just wanted directions, and she seemed to want to talk about the meaning of life. She was quirky. Interesting. But he didn't have time for her now. He had a climb to get to and a job to do.

"Look," he said, "if the only thing you're worried about today is a confusing signpost, you're lucky. I'm way past that point. I just need to know the shortest path to reach that mountain. Can you help me?"

"I do want to help. Let me try to explain it another way. I'm just saying there are many paths to find what you're looking for. Anxiety is believing there is only one."

He felt a tiny tug. There was certainly a truth there.

She sensed his interest and continued. "When you're looking for *the* path, most of them will feel wrong. When you're looking for *any* path, then almost all of them will feel right."

His instinct was to debate, to find the exceptions, but he decided to listen for a change. He knew what it felt like to become obsessed with just one path. He thought of Claudia, the girl he'd thought was the only one for him. Losing her had hurt him deeply.

"We're told from an early age that we need to choose a path," the girl said. "As children, people ask us what we want to be when we grow up, as if there's an endpoint in life to aim for. They tell us we can become whatever we want, if we just pursue it hard enough. We watch movies about heroes who start with a dream and pursue it with unwavering commitment to the very end. But in reality, for every hero who reaches their goal, there are hundreds of anxious souls who fail."

"What's your solution? To just wander down any random path in life?"

"Not random. But, yes, you can choose to walk life one path at a time. Cross the river by feeling the stones. Take a path to reach the next crossroads. Just never fixate on the final destination. Many people prefer dirt paths to paved ones and see life as an endless series of walks to be enjoyed."

"Not all who wander are lost, then?" the boy joked weakly. It was the only Tolkien line he knew. She seemed so confident about everything, perched up on her rock, he thought, but he wasn't buying it all.

"I'm sorry," he said, "but I couldn't live my life like that, with no end point, no direction, no meaning."

"Having no fixed end point is not the same as having no meaning. We worry far too much about the path we take and not enough about the way we walk it. The way we walk it creates a meaningful life, not the destination. Too many people live restlessly, searching for their special purpose, anxious they'll never find it. Or when they *think* they've found it, they live in fear of losing it. But happiness is always right there in front of us if we want it. We just need to focus on the *way* we walk—the *how*—and not the destination."

He'd heard enough. She was interesting, but he had to move on. She seemed to have an agenda, and he didn't have the time to find out what it was. "Well, it seems to be working for you, even if it's not the right philosophy for me. Thank you for the lecture." More than a little sarcasm crept into his voice. "I'm sure you'll live a long and happy life wandering in the meadows."

He nodded goodbye and turned away, striking out on the path heading toward the highest mountain.

Eyes down, shallow breaths, tight lips.

"Au revoir!" the girl called after him. "Goodbye, again," she added softly.

The Guide

The boy kicked rocks for a mile down the dirt path. From the moment he'd left the girl sitting on her boulder, he regretted the way he'd ended the conversation. She was just trying to help, and she might be the last person he would meet before his climb. His words to her could be his last. What was it that Claudia used to say to him? "Not every conversation needs to be a debate."

And what if the girl was right? He *was* always looking for perfection. He'd spent his whole life searching for the right path, never stopping to enjoy life. Maybe that was his problem.

Oh, and, sure, she was undeniably beautiful…

Wait, my flask!

He had dropped it back at the crossroads. He had to go back for it. He sprinted back down the path with renewed energy.

The girl still sat on her boulder. Her long lashes were shut, and she had her face to the sun. She was meditating. She sat still like an ancient statue that had always belonged there.

He waited for her to look down at him, but she was in deep repose. He wanted to talk to her again, but he wanted her to speak first. He scraped his feet over to the metal flask and picked it up. He then pretended to drop it, and it clanged at his feet on the path. Surely, she'd heard that!

She sat in perfect stillness. He'd have to be the one to break the silence.

"Sorry, it's me again. I forgot my flask."

She opened her eyes and smiled down at him.

"While I'm here," he continued, "I also want to say sorry for the way I talked to you earlier and for walking off like that. I'm not good at taking advice. I'm told I'm a terrible listener."

She nodded, still smiling.

Oh, God, she's giving me the silent treatment.

"I've also been thinking about what you said, about choosing paths, and I think you're probably right. Choosing does make me anxious. I've always worried about whether I'm on the right path or not. Maybe I've been worrying about the wrong things all my life. Maybe the *way* we live our life *is* the meaning."

"Yes!" she cried. She sprang to her feet and clambered down the boulder. "I'm coming down to congratulate you now. That's quite a breakthrough statement."

He felt a leap of pride. He was still grinning as she pulled herself in for a short but surprising hug. Up close, she was much shorter than he'd expected—and even more beautiful.

"I like it when you smile," she said. "You should do it more often. You were designed to smile. It tells me you have something to give or share."

"I was hoping *you* might have something more to share. I wish I'd met you a few months ago. You seem to have life all figured out."

"Who me?" she said. "I'm sorry if I gave that impression. I can assure you I'm still figuring most things out myself."

He was disappointed but asked again anyway. "Just one piece of advice would help right now. Anything."

She thought hard. "I see this smile on your face. You're already feeling lighter. Just step aside and get out of the way. That's all you need to do. The most beautiful parts of you shine when you get out of the way."

He didn't know why he was smiling so much. To his relief, she continued.

"Modern life makes us mad. It's like we've built a madhouse for our minds and thrown away the key. Junk food, junk media, junk jobs, junk substances, junk values. Impossible expectations, endless interruptions, and conflicting choices. Most people don't see all this junk and live happily enough. But if you think deeply and worry about things, you'll end up as mad as a rabid dog chasing its tail."

"Woof!" he barked.

She laughed. "Exhibit A."

He became serious again. "I wish I could ignore it, but I think too hard about everything. All the things you mentioned: I'm exhausted by it all. I've spent my whole life trying to find happiness, and I can't keep searching like this. Unless you know of a book with all the answers in it, I'm lost."

He felt he had nothing to lose. He found it easy to open up to her. As she stood still, thinking hard, he noticed she wore many bracelets. He counted more than a dozen on each arm, some silver, some just a single colored thread, all hinting at a story from another land.

"Well, I don't have a book, but I probably do have a few chapters," she said. "I've also searched for many years, just like you, and I went out into the world to find answers. I met teachers, read a lot, studied different religions and science. I slowly started to piece everything together in a way that made sense for me. I'd always wanted a guide to live a good life, but it had to be something I believed in and simple enough to follow every day. I originally thought I was looking for something that already existed, but, in the end, I had to weave it myself, like a magpie's nest. I made my own guide, and you could make yours too if you set aside the time."

"I've run out of time," he said sadly. "Will you share yours with me?" He was still grasping for a way out.

"Sorry, I don't know how to. It's not written down. It's all in my head."

"Try me, please."

"I've tried explaining it to people before, but it never ends well."

"It can't end worse than what I'm planning," he said darkly.

"Don't joke about that."

"I'm not."

"Then you're dumber than you look."

"Oh, I'm far dumber. Just try me, please."

She groaned. "You never give up, do you?"

"I promise I'll listen. I learn fast."

"OK. I'll share a few ideas. Just a few. You seem smart. Once you've listened to me for a while, you'll want to go and write your own guide anyway, like I did. We can walk and talk a bit in the meadow before going our separate ways. Deal?"

"Deal!"

"Wait, I don't even know your name!" They shook hands and introduced themselves.

She thought for a moment, then picked up a sturdy stick. She pointed to a patch of dirt out in the sunlight.

"There's a framework I use. It's easier if I draw it for you."

She began carving out a simple triangle in the sunbaked earth. She then split it into three segments, humming as she sketched.

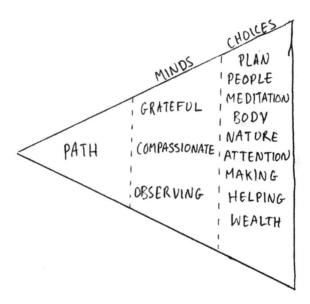

TAKE A PATH AND WALK IT WITH
A GOOD MIND AND GOOD CHOICES.

"It's very simple," she said. She tapped the sharp segment on the left side of the triangle. "This part represents the path." She then tapped the middle segment. "These are the three minds." Finally, she tapped the broad segment on the right side. "These are our choices. There are nine. To flourish, we must take a path and walk it with a good mind and making good choices. Then we get out of the way. That's it."

"Wait. That's it?"

"That's it. A guide to the good life. I told you it was simple."

He didn't know what he'd expected, but it was something more than this. "What are these minds? And what are the choices?"

"Three minds. Nine choices." She started to etch the names into the earth, gently nudging an unsuspecting beetle away from the grooves. "First, we must always try to walk with three minds: the grateful mind, the compassionate mind, and the observing mind."

"How do they all work?"

"Think of them as *the way* you walk your path, or *how* you walk it. You can't control most things in life, but you can strengthen these three minds like building muscles in a gym. In fact, just like muscles, it's a good idea to keep strengthening them your whole life, right to the end. They protect you from all the junk the world hits you with. With a mind that is grateful, compassionate, and observing, you can create the world you live in. We think we see the world as it is, but we actually see it as we are."

He was hooked. He stared down at the three words while she spoke. He wanted to know how to build each mind, but she was already moving on.

"Now remember, take a path and walk it with a good mind and by making nine good choices. We must make good choices every day. This is never easy because we often have less control over these than we have over our own mindset. But over time our choices become habits, which are easier to manage. This makes it all simpler. As choices become habits, we create grooves in our minds, as our neurons fire and wire together, and the grooves eventually get deeper and easier to follow."

"So why not call them habits?"

"I always call them choices to remind myself how hard-fought they are and how the responsibility always lies with me. The freedom to make these choices is what separates us from animals and machines. Walking a path is not something to believe in; it's something to do."

She sang each of the choices out as she etched them into the dirt:

- Choice of Plan
- Choice of People
- Choice of Meditation
- Choice of Body
- Choice of Nature
- Choice of Attention
- Choice of Making
- Choice of Helping
- Choice of Wealth

He was mesmerized. She had the certainty and conviction of a child.

"Why are there nine of them? Why not eight or ten? And why this order?"

"No reason, no order. These are mine. You can write your own. Just start by starting. I started with three, then I had four, then five, and now I've built up to nine. I've studied each one deeply and developed habits around them, although I don't have time to go into them all now. Sometimes I pick one of the nine choices to focus on for the day. And at night, before I fall asleep, I usually review all of them in my mind."

He stared down at the triangle for a moment and then thanked her.

"It looked simple at first, but now I can see how much thinking lies behind it," he said. "Do you mind if I sketch it out in my notepad before we walk on?" With sadness, he thought it was a shame he'd never get to learn the guide fully.

As he sketched, she hummed softly behind him.

Then the humming stopped.

"Look!" she whispered. "We have a friend."

He looked up to see a majestic fourteen-point stag watching them intently from behind the trunk of a sequoia. Two fearless black eyes were fixed on them, just twenty feet away. Everything stopped. Nobody breathed. Impossibly, the deer stepped forward, tiptoeing elegantly right between them, and continued on into the forest.

It felt like he'd been holding his breath forever. And then he felt a release of joy.

"Did that really just happen?" he asked.

She shook her head in disbelief.

"Surely that's a sign." He laughed, clutching his red Moleskin notepad. "You were meant to be my teacher!"

"You have no idea how much this changes things," she said quietly. She hoisted her pack onto her shoulder and led the way down the middle path. "Let's go. Let's talk."

The Grateful Mind

They walked side by side in silence under the afternoon sun.

"I can share a few ways to develop your grateful mind," the girl said.

She stopped and pulled out an apple from her pocket. She cut two slices with her knife, and they placed them gently on their tongues. She then showed him how to walk more slowly than he had ever imagined: five steps in five minutes. They noted only the sweet taste and texture of the apple's flesh. They savored each subtle element of the flavor and felt grateful for it.

Finally, he broke the silence. "That was intense!"

They erupted in laughter.

"You see, most people get it wrong," she said. "Gratitude creates happiness, not the other way around. It's like a muscle you need to flex. The more you give your grateful mind a workout, the happier you'll be. It's about feeling lucky. Luck is believing you're lucky. The happiest people learn to feel lucky *while* they're happy, not only after it has passed."

"I enjoyed savoring the apple. Are there other exercises like that?"

She told him about the reframing exercises that Roman

Stoic philosophers such as Seneca and Marcus Aurelius had written about more than two thousand years ago.

"One's called negative visualization. This is where you imagine all the things that could possibly go wrong, or all the things that could be taken away from you, in advance before it can take you by surprise. As Seneca said, 'The unexpected blows of fortune fall heaviest and most painfully, which is why the wise man anticipates them.'

"Another is voluntary discomfort. This goes one step further to actually embrace hardship before it happens. For example, Cato the Younger was a Roman senator who would walk around Rome in unusual clothing so people would laugh at him. He walked barefoot and without a hat in the midday sun and in the rain, and he rationed his diet to prepare for hardship."

"That reminds me of a book I read about wandering Buddhist monks in Burma," he said. "They never slept more than three nights in any one place their whole lives. That way they never become too comfortable."

"Exactly! My favorite Stoic exercise is called 'the last time.' Here you imagine that what you do today—this walk, this talk, that slice of apple—you will do for the very last time. Imagine how you will savor it, feel grateful for it."

The boy flinched when she said 'the last time', and he tried to avoid her eyes. He was enjoying the conversation and didn't want to think about his lonely climb up to the cliff-face. That would come later.

"Do you know any techniques that aren't two thousand years old?" he asked.

"Sure, you could try to keep a gratitude journal. Just write down everything you're grateful for at the end of the day. There should always be a lot to write if you remember that someone somewhere is praying for what you take for granted. It's clinically proven that writing a gratitude journal makes people happier."

"Evenings aren't a problem for me. It's the mornings. I wake up every morning with intense anxiety, even when my life is going well. It comes in fast like a thick, dark fog. Then it finds something to latch onto, and I can lose the whole morning."

"I used to get morning anxiety too, but I learned a simple gratitude trick to clear it. It takes only thirty seconds if you do it right. Close your eyes now and think of three things you can permanently feel grateful for."

"OK."

"Now write them down."

He did.

"Now, whenever you wake up and that dark mist descends on you, just immediately think of these three things. Think about them fast before the anxiety gets started. Stick with the same three. Don't try to change them. The anxiety should dissolve when you do this."

"Why?"

"Because it will have nothing to feed on if you're lying there feeling grateful."

He decided to try it the next morning, but he still had questions. "I've learned a lot about gratitude today. I'm sure I can build it up like a muscle over time, but I'm not sure it can help with the really deep sadness."

"Go on."

"Look, I'm dealing with some deep-down sadness right now. You know, some real my-pa-died-and-my-woman-gone-and-left-me kind of sadness. In other words, I'm not sure how to feel grateful. I mean, I can dance around this stuff and put on a brave face, but it's all still going to be weighing down on me."

"Believe it or not, you really can and should feel grateful about all of it. And I mean all of it. Life is just a series of doors that open and close for us. When we're hurt, and somebody slams a door in our face, we get so angry we can't notice all the new doors that open up. Just think of it as a door that *had to close first* before a new one could open up. Try to feel grateful that a new door can open up. Like me. I'm your newest door, aren't I?"

He smiled at her, feeling grateful. "I guess you are."

She laughed, miming a door opening. "I'm sure another door had to close before you could find me."

"You could say that."

"Then I believe that's all I have to share about the grateful mind."

"Sure, but what's your principle? What do I write in my notebook to remember it all?"

"My principle?"

"You need to boil it all down into a single line. A precise and crisp statement. That way you can always teach it to idiots like me."

"I see. Well, I have no idea. I've never tried to teach idiots like you. It sounds hard."

He thought about it for a minute, scribbling things down and crossing things out in his notebook. Then finally he read it out loud: "'The grateful mind: Savor it all, every day, and always feel lucky.' What do you think?"

"I think you're good at this. I like it. I might need to keep you around!"

She saluted him, and he noticed a small but bright tattoo on her wrist. "Is that a hummingbird?" he asked. "I just saw one in the meadow. It's beautiful."

"Thank you. Yes, she's my little reminder to be grateful." She briefly bared her wrist, then folded her arms.

"Grateful for…"

She looked down at the ground quietly. "For the chance to start again. For rebirth. The hummingbird has been a symbol of self-discovery, of love and many things, for thousands of years. And across many different cultures. The Aztecs believed that if they died in battle, they would be reincarnated as hummingbirds. The Hopi and Zuni believed they spoke to the gods to bring rain when needed. If you study them in slow motion, a hummingbird's wings make the shape of an infinity loop when they flap."

She paused to find words. "There was a time when I needed to kill off parts of my life in order to start again. She reminds me of that time and that chance I got."

She looked up again and they both smiled. He thanked her and they walked on, side by side.

The Compassionate Mind

The path snaked tightly beside the stream. The track narrowed, so they walked single file, the girl humming softly ahead of the boy. An older couple approached them from the opposite direction, making their way along the stream with walking poles in their hands and their heads down. The girl greeted them warmly, but they barely looked up as they brushed by and marched on without a word.

"Nice to meet you too," the boy called after them angrily. "Unbelievable!"

Half a mile farther down the path, they found two empty plastic bottles and a brown paper bag scattered next to a giant log.

"No way!" the boy cried angrily. "Did that old couple just dump their trash here in the meadow? What's their problem? I should run after them and stuff it into their backpacks."

"Look," the girl said, "they also left a wallet on the log. They must have left it while they were eating here." She grabbed the wallet. "Wait here. I need to get it back to them."

Before he could stop her, she was running back down the

path and was soon out of sight. It was more than twenty minutes before she returned, panting but grinning.

"I can't believe you just did that," the boy said. "Who does that? Seriously, nobody does that. The two rudest jerks on the mountain, and you left me here standing around like an idiot while you ran a whole mile to return their wallet to them. I just hope they were very grateful."

She picked up the trash and stuffed it into her bag. "Yes, they were grateful. And embarrassed. I told them we'd also clean up their trash.

"You did?"

"Yes, and they apologized a lot. I could see they were struggling with some sadness in their lives. Didn't you notice it on their faces when they walked past us?"

He shook his head in disbelief. "No, I just saw two rude people and their angry faces. But perhaps I saw only what I was looking for. That's a big difference between you and me. This feels like a great time for me to start learning about the compassionate mind, because I'm still struggling with what just happened."

The girl laughed and agreed. She suggested they keep walking while she gathered her thoughts.

"What do you think of when you hear the word *compassion*?" she asked him after a while.

"The Dalai Lama. I wrote a quote of his in my eighth-grade yearbook: 'If you want others to be happy, practice compassion. If you want to be happy, practice compassion.' I haven't forgotten the quote, but I feel I've forgotten what it meant along the way."

"Exactly. That's a perfect place to start. If your compassion makes others happy, you will be happy. This is part of the virtuous circle of the compassionate mind. It's a very simple circle. It starts with self-love. You must love yourself first before you can love others. Being kind to yourself empowers you to act kindly toward others, which in turn makes you love yourself even more. You see how it works?"

"Again, please."

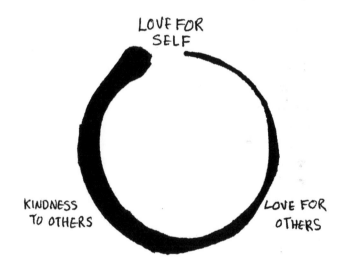

LOVE FOR SELF

KINDNESS TO OTHERS

LOVE FOR OTHERS

COMPASSIONATE MIND: WE MUST CARE AND DO MORE IF POSSIBLE, AND IT'S ALWAYS POSSIBLE.

"OK, draw a clock in your mind with just three times of day: love for self, love for others, and kindness to others. You start with self-love, and around and around it goes forever in an infinite loop. Love and compassion have no limits. See it now?"

"I see it, but I'm afraid I don't live it. You're saying that acts of kindness for others are what make us love ourselves? Empathy alone isn't enough?"

"Empathy is feeling what others feel. Compassion is putting yourself in another person's shoes as a way to help ease their suffering. For example, imagine you're trekking across this meadow and you find a girl pinned beneath a boulder. Empathy would mean feeling the same sense of pain and suffocation as her, which might render you helpless. A compassionate trekker, however, would recognize her suffering and make all the efforts necessary to remove the boulder and ease it."

"So, compassion isn't just a feeling."

"Compassion is empathy plus action."

Good. He always found equations easy to remember: COMPASSION = EMPATHY + ACTION.

"It all sounds too simple," he said. "If it were this easy, shouldn't we all be drowning in compassionate bliss by now?"

"I've met many people who are. But, yes, we all should be. Unfortunately, our species has a few design flaws we need to work on. Regardless, the science on compassion all checks out. The positive chemical effects of being kind are well documented. When we act out of kindness, we experience a 'helper's high,' a surge of endorphins associated with euphoria. You get a warm feeling when practicing compassion, as it releases oxytocin. This is a hormone that helps us bond with others, and it appears to reduce heart disease."

"There's really all of this science behind it?"

"Sure. Even brain scans of Buddhist monks show physical differences compared to the average person. The effects of compassion are real and measurable. People are starting to accept these facts. Companies are even investing in it."

"This all sounds too good to be true. I don't think the world would function properly if we all went around just being kind to each other."

"Wouldn't it? Imagine a world where everyone puts kindness first. Even simple words can be powerful. A few kind words can make a big difference in someone's life. Try to remember the last time you gave the gift of kindness to somebody."

As hard as he tried, he couldn't remember a single moment in the past year when he was kind to someone.

Perhaps sensing he was struggling, the girl said, "Was there a time when you listened to somebody? When you truly and fully just listened to them? Kind listening can be as powerful as kind words or actions."

Again, nothing.

He had always tried to be the smartest person in the room. It never occurred to him to be the kindest. No wonder no one ever said kind words to him. He hadn't earned them.

"Look, don't be so hard on yourself," she said. "It's easy to beat yourself up, and it just makes it harder to get your circle of compassion going. The first object of your love must be yourself. If you can't first love yourself, you won't ever have enough love to give to others. To become a fountain instead of a drain, you must love and accept yourself fully."

She was asking him to start loving himself. He didn't even know how to stop hating himself.

"It's hard," she said. "We all screw this up, a dozen times a day. We're all in our own bubble. The people we love the most are often the ones we neglect the most. Everyone's fighting a lonely battle, a battle we usually know nothing about. A little kindness always helps. We can all do better."

"But how do I get started? I want a compassionate mind."

She smiled. "Does that mean you want to run after rude people to help them?"

"Touché! Yes, I guess I do."

"OK, then, just open yourself up and get out of the way. Always err on the side of kindness. Simply follow the circle: love for self, love for others, kindness to others, then more love for self. When someone makes you happy, make them happier."

She then gave him some advice for dealing with his dark mornings. She suggested he get a pet or a plant so his first act every morning would be unselfish.

"A pet? That's a big commitment," he joked.

"Start with a cactus. They don't need much water."

"Seriously though. There's one problem. I don't think I even know how to love myself. Can I start by being kind to others? Can self-love grow from there?"

"Sure."

"Would you like to know the line I'm going to use to remember all of this?"

She nodded.

"'The compassionate mind: We must care and do more if possible, and it's always possible.'"

"That's perfect. You like to write things down, don't you?"

"I have to, or I'd go mad. If I don't write down my last idea, I can't move on to the next one. My brain is a useless place to store old ideas but a great place to think about new ones."

"I like that. It's important to try to understand your brain."

The girl turned and set off down the path once again. "Let's walk!"

A Boy

A boy stood at his bedroom window and looked down at the neighborhood kids dressed in costumes. Batman, a mermaid, and three zombies ran past holding hands. Kids roamed in groups, clutching bags of candy, shouting and laughing through the darkness. The boy watched from the window, sketching random shapes, making up his mind.

"Mom, Dad, can I do Halloween this year?"

Silence.

Then his father's voice from downstairs: "Hey, T, we talked about this last year, right? We're not a Halloween family. It's no big deal. It's Thanksgiving soon, anyway."

The boy stood at the window with a notepad and a well-chewed pencil and kept sketching. "But I really want to do it this year. I think my friends are out there. I can see them. I can go on my own, like the other kids."

Parents' whispers.

Then: "Sorry, T, we don't have costumes, I'm afraid. Next year we'll do it. We can get costumes."

"I could make my own. I can be a ghost in a sheet. It's easy. I can go on my own. I don't mind doing it on my own."

Louder whispers.

This time his mother: "I'm sorry, T, we're not comfortable with it. Some very strange people out there, especially tonight. They put poison in the candy. It's not safe…"

"And we don't even eat candy in this house, do we?" his father added. "What would you do with it all?"

"It's a school night, darling. If you're drawing up there again, put it away now. You have your homework to finish. That's your priority, not dressing up and scaring people."

The boy closed his notepad and looked out the window.

Chewbacca looked up from the street and waved at him.

He waved back.

The Observing Mind

"Would this make a good campsite for the night?" the boy called out, signaling to a gentle slope ahead.

They'd walked in silence for most of the afternoon, and he still didn't know how long she would stick around.

"It's good, not great," she called back without turning. "Keep looking for a clearing, near some dry firewood and within sight of the stream. Just not too close. The storms and lightning come in fast overnight, so don't pitch up next to any trees. Look for clusters of boulders. They break up the wind. Watch out for poison oak, too, or ledges where snakes might be hiding out. Oh, and avoid falling rocks."

She enjoyed giving orders, he thought.

He found another spot a mile farther down the path, and she agreed it was ideal. He leaned his pack up against a boulder and started collecting firewood, while she filled their flasks at the stream and added tablets.

She offered to help pitch his tent, but he wanted to do it himself. Before he'd gotten his tent poles connected, she'd already hitched her hammock between two trees and tested it out. She then took a seat below a nearby tree, facing the setting sun, and began to meditate.

Eventually he pitched the tent and his fire crackled and smoked. He boiled water for tea and heated up a can of beans. He looked over at the girl meditating by the tree. The final rays of sunset gilded her body's outline, framing her upright posture with a warm glow.

He'd never meditated. It always gave him the creeps, and he hoped she wouldn't try to make him do it. He found her captivating, though. Self-assured. She didn't seem to need anybody.

Perhaps she was too self-assured.

She sat in stillness for an hour and then slowly rose to her feet. She seemed to say a few words to the tree before walking to the fire with a smile.

"A campfire needs a story," she said. "Are you ready to discuss the observing mind?"

"My mind and book are open, and my pen is ready," the boy said. "The observing mind. I feel I need one. What is it? Why do we want it? How do we get it?"

"I'll answer all three, but I have some questions for you first. Have you ever noticed how long it takes to calm down after you get angry or jealous? Even when you can barely remember the original cause of the feeling? And have you noticed that the anger feeds off itself like a fire raging through a building? All out of control, all from a mere spark?"

He nodded because he had on both counts.

"And have you noticed that the things you crave, even when you attain them, cause you to crave them even more, whether it's sugar, alcohol, drugs, money, success, or affection? Have you noticed how they lead to stronger cravings and never to satisfaction? Craving leads to an endless wheel of needing, and when we finally get what we crave, we cling to it for dear life, living in constant fear of losing it."

He was impressed. "Sure, I've noticed all of these things before, but isn't it the same for everyone? Isn't this simply what it means to be human?"

"It is, and perhaps it's the tragedy at the heart of the human condition. Our brains have developed through millennia of evolution, but this hasn't helped us shape our minds to see the world clearly. Rather, it has geared us toward taking care of and passing on our genes. It's the result of a world of scarcity, back in a time when it made sense to gorge ourselves on anything we could find. See a berry? Eat it. See a whole bush of berries? Eat them all. See anything that gives you pleasure? Take it. Take all of it. Our ancestors never knew when their next meal might come along."

The boy nodded, but where was she was going with all of this?

"In fact, the pleasures we crave and the aversions that disgust us have been coded in our brains by the evolutionary process. Just think how pleasure evaporates almost instantly, making us feel dissatisfied and wanting even more pleasure. This evolutionary behavioral process is an algorithm that doesn't care about our happiness; it just cares about our productivity. It uses us. It makes the anticipation of pleasure very strong even if the pleasure itself lasts only a few seconds. It always leaves us wanting more. This is the tragedy of our condition."

"You're saying we're programmed to be unhappy then? That's pretty bleak."

"Yes, we're wired this way, but it doesn't need to be our

destiny. We're born with our brains running this program, but we *can* rewrite our code."

"Really? How?"

"That's why we need an observing mind. If we sit back and allow all of these reactions to take place—the cravings and the aversions—they will always control us. But if we learn to observe our feelings mindfully rather than react to them, we can start to escape their control. We can break down our regular patterns of suffering. The sparks no longer become raging fires, and the cravings no longer eat us up. To break the old circuits and rewrite the code, we need an observing mind. This mind doesn't get distracted; it sees things as they really are. And if we develop a calmer and clearer mind, it will lead to better decisions and ultimately a happier life."

She paused and smiled at him across the campfire. She looked more than a little impressed by her succinct explanation.

He was less impressed. It all sounded fluffy to him.

"I can see how sure you feel about all of this," he said, "but can we slow things down a bit? This is all very new to me. Can we go back to my three questions about the observing mind?

"Sure. Let's slow down and look at each of your questions."

As she spoke, he distilled her answers in his notebook.

> *What is it?* It's neither chasing nor avoiding things but simply noting them and being there in the middle.

> *Why do we want it?* Because a calm mind sees things clearly and makes good decisions. A calm mind is our best mind.

How do we get it? By practicing meditation and studying our own mind.

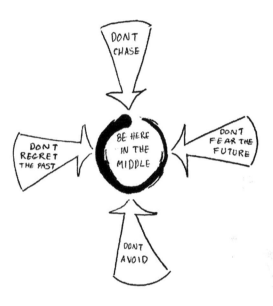

OBSERVING MIND

DONT CHASE

DONT REGRET THE PAST

BE HERE IN THE MIDDLE

DONT FEAR THE FUTURE

DONT AVOID

A CALM MIND SEES THINGS CLEARLY AND MAKES GOOD DECISIONS.

A CALM MIND IS OUR BEST MIND.

It was starting to make a little more sense, but he had more questions.

"Do I have to learn to meditate to develop an observing mind?" he asked.

"I don't know any other way. Meditation is hard work, but it's simple to learn and it works. When I meditate, I sit still and look *into* my mind instead of looking *out* from it. I practice observing and accepting my thoughts without reacting to them. And when we understand the way we see things, the way we see things will change."

"What exactly does the mind observe?"

"It notices and accepts how good things and bad things come and go, naturally and endlessly. It sees that all bad things must come to an end. It watches how the mind jumps from past regrets to future anxiety without enjoying the present moment. It observes that we don't control our own thoughts; they think themselves. It learns how the mind looks for something to grab onto and feed off of. The observing mind notes all of these things and accepts them."

"Slow down, please. This is all good stuff. It sounds like a disease, a madness. How does the mind stay sane?"

"When the observing mind sees thoughts that are incorrect, it stops identifying with them. It notes them and moves on to calmness."

"But what if it doesn't work? What if you just make things worse by trying to observe your own thoughts?"

"That will happen a lot at first. A child learning to ride a bike might fall and get hurt a dozen times before getting it right. When you begin, your brain will be hijacked by thoughts acting like gangs of thieves. They will flood in and ransack the cupboards of your mind. In the time of Buddha, they called this the proliferating mind, which describes how our thoughts multiply and take on disproportionate importance. But if you practice regularly, you will learn to see them coming. Your cupboards will be empty. Those thoughts will become thieves in an empty house."

He wanted to understand this and believe her, but he was getting tired.

"I'm listening," he sighed, "but I'm struggling with it. It's getting late."

"It's OK. I'm tired too. What part confuses you?"

"I don't think I want my cupboards to be empty. It just sounds like doing nothing, thinking nothing. It sounds like indifference or withdrawal. How can you ever get anything done with an empty mind?"

"That's a fair question, but I would turn it back to you. How can you ever get anything done with a stormy mind?"

"Maybe it's good to feel passionate about things," he argued. "It's part of the creative process. To have fire in the belly. I feel more motivated when I'm all fired up."

"The Buddha called anger a lump of hot coal you hold in your hand while waiting to throw it at someone. Creativity is very rarely born out of anger, but it's often stifled and narrowed by it. Anger steals the most valuable thing in the world: our time. When someone upsets us, it takes only ten seconds for anger to steal the other eighty thousand seconds of the day."

If she wanted an argument, he was ready for it, he thought. "That's not always true. All the successful people I know and the celebrities I follow—they all have a passion, a view about the world. They *do* get angry. They *do* have enemies. They *do* feel things. They have real stories. That's what makes them stand out. And I want to stand out. I'm tired of being ignored. This just feels weak. And odd. I'd feel embarrassed to tell people I'm just observing my thoughts, not using my brain to think new ones."

She paused for a moment before answering him. Her face was lit up by the fire, and the black mountain sky framed it. "What other people think of you is none of your business. Your value doesn't decrease based on their inability to see your worth."

He shrugged. "Look, you might not care what others think of you, but I do. I guess we can agree to disagree on that."

"I think we often care too much about what others think of us, and that's often the main obstacle to our happiness. Can I ask you one more thing tonight before you sleep?"

"Sure."

"When you were young, whose love did you crave the most? Who did you have to be to win that love?"

The question hung there in the darkness, and it was impossible to ignore. He hadn't thought about his father all day, but now he felt the gaze of his haunting eyes.

"Whoa," he said. "That's a heavy one. I'm not even sure." A thousand frames flashed through his mind, scrolling through childhood memories of his serious father and his anxious mother. "I guess my father. His was the love I craved the most, before he died. But we never really *did* love at my house. It was there, but it went unspoken. I knew he was there for me if I ever needed him. He always had my back."

"I'm sorry. I didn't know you lost your father."

"Thanks, it's fine," he lied. "Apparently it's better to talk about these things." He absolutely did not want to talk about it with her, not now.

"And who did you need to be for him?"

"Who did I need to be? I don't even know. He never told me. I don't think about it."

"I think we all know deep down."

He felt a spark.

"Hey, hold on now," he said, feeling rising anger. "You don't know. You don't know me. You don't know him. You don't know everything." He choked a little. "Sure, you have answers for everything under the sun, and it's very impressive, but you don't know me."

Rising, louder.

"In fact, walking with you today has left me more confused than when I started out. I thought you had all the answers, but you clearly don't. It's all been…just noise…so far. A total waste of time."

The girl had crossed a line. He was standing over her now, seething.

"Thank you, and all that. I'm probably a bit tired, so sorry for raising my voice. But you really don't know me. How could you? We just met. You don't know my problems. I'm not you, and you're certainly not me. I'm heading to bed. Good night."

Without looking up, he stepped away from the fire and into the darkness. He stumbled over to his tent and crawled inside, zipping it closed behind him.

The Forest

The boy lay seething in his tent, staring at the glow of the moonlight through the blue fabric.

He could feel himself slowly exploding.

Fast, heavy breaths. Chest thumping. Ears ringing. Palms sweating.

He wanted to burst out of the tent and walk it off, but he couldn't face talking to her again. She had crossed a line, and he didn't trust himself not to flare up if she was still out by the fire. He had come to the mountain to get a job done, and she was distracting him.

The memories of the foggy nights on the bridge flooded back to him. The red flakes of paint, the cold steel, the salty nostrils.

It was time. He was ready again.

The silence in the tent was deafening. He could walk out right now, right past her, and start climbing the nearest cliff. He didn't need to reach the thousand-foot monolith at the end of the valley; a hundred feet fall would do the job just fine. There was a decent granite wall on the other side of the forest. He pulled the zipper open and crawled out into the chilly night air, relieved to see she was gone.

She probably never planned to camp with him anyway, he thought.

The embers hissed, and the moonlight laid a silver track across the meadow to the forest's edge. He rubbed his hands over the remains of the fire for a minute before setting off toward the trees.

As he walked past the first row of firs, his mind replayed the last conversation by the fire.

Why had she started talking about his parents? Why make it so personal, and challenging, when she didn't even know him? She had asked whose love he craved, who he needed to be to please them. What kind of questions are those anyway? His parents had never told him he had to go to Stanford; he'd pushed himself. They hadn't forced him to do anything. It was his decision to aim high and make all the sacrifices.

Enough. It's over.

As he walked deeper into the forest, the trees grew thicker and the moonlight became dimmer. A well-trodden path had led him into the forest, but it continued to dwindle away between the trunks. He kicked at rotting logs and raised his elbows to shield his eyes from branches that reached across what was left of the path. The temperature had dropped, and he wished he'd brought his jacket and gloves. It would be hard to climb the wall with icy fingers. His heart was thumping again, but this time it was out of fear and excitement, not anger.

After a while, he started to hit thicker clusters of underbrush, and thorny brambles snared his sweater. He was stuck. He would have to turn back and find another path. In a fit of frustration, he kicked through one last wall of branches, and it opened into a tiny glade.

The clearing was improbably lit. He crawled through the gap to get a better look. The moonlight shone through the sparse canopy above. He threw his arms out wide and spun around and around, bathing in the silver light as if on stage under a spotlight. The glade was like a secret garden built just for him. He laughed at the oddness of it all, then broke into a coughing fit.

He was chilled to the bones. He needed to keep moving.

Turning to crawl back through the gap, he noticed a perfect ring of slender brown mushrooms at his feet. He kneeled down to inspect them closer and plucked the smallest from the ring. He held it up against the moonlight and twisted it between his thumb and forefinger. There was no mistaking the long, drooping bell shape. He'd read all about them. Psilocybin mushrooms. Psychedelic mushrooms. Magic mushrooms. *Shrooms*. Used in ancient rituals by cultures all over the world to liberate the mind, they were powerfully hallucinogenic.

Why not? What did he have to lose?

"Not a bad way to go," he reasoned, "falling off a cliff with a smile on my face…"

It felt like a sign. It made things much easier.

Still on his knees, he plucked a dozen mushrooms with his icy fingers and scooped them into his sweater pocket. He started to step back through the gap and then paused for a moment. They'd take a while to kick in. Why not take one or two now so the effects would kick in when he started climbing? He pulled out two mushrooms from his pocket, dusted them off carefully and swallowed them whole, his teeth chattering in the chilly air.

Now he had to backtrack and find a way through the forest

to the rock face. He set off, hacking through the forest, groping his way back. He should have brought his coat. He was crazy not to. The route back should have been simple, but it wasn't clear now. He kicked his way through logs and branches, but he wasn't sure which way he was heading anymore.

The branches kept snagging him. Very frustrating... It was colder than he'd expected. Must be the mountain air, the altitude. He was lightheaded and sneezing often, uncontrollably. Eight times. He'd been walking for a while, maybe twenty minutes. Or more. He should be reaching the meadow soon.

He thought about the warmth of the fire... Another bout of sneezing... God, it was cold...stupidly cold... His gut was aching now...a long, dull ache...cold and aching in his gut, all over...might vomit...sweating and dizzy...

Yes, he was definitely going to vomit... Better out than in... Probably the mushrooms... Should not have eaten two... Maybe he was wrong about them...maybe poisonous... He could die here... He should vomit... Better to lie down for a bit here...but cold...very, very cold now...

Three tall, white-haired men wearing togas met with three robed monks at a crossroads at night in a meadow.

They stood in silence beside a roaring fire, roasting giant mushrooms.

The flames danced up to their shoulders, throwing up a smoky blue pillar.

A boy approached from the meadow, and they pointed him toward a white tent decorated with colorful prayer flags.

A giant zipper opened silently as he approached the tent.

He stopped, and the zipper stopped.

He stepped forward, and the zipper opened until he reached the entrance and fell inside, pushed from behind.

Outside, the men were chanting now, words he didn't understand. A gong chimed at the end of every line.

His mother sat inside the tent, smiling and laughing, but she was young, about his age. She held him tightly in her arms. She whispered to him and sang.

The tent slowly filled with tiny hummingbirds, their iridescent wings flapping against the white canvas. All the colorful wings buzzed together, fast at first, and then slowed to a rhythmic throb.

He reached up to touch his head and found it had grown like a giant balloon, filling the whole tent. There was a hole from which all the vibrant birds were streaming out, some as tiny as bees, making him laugh uncontrollably.

His mother held him tightly, eyes bright and soft, and hushed him.

Hushed him until he slept.

Her Story

"Knock, knock!"

The boy opened his eyes. He was back inside his tent, snug inside a sleeping bag.

"Good morning! Knock, knock!

"Who's there?" he croaked. It was the only question he *did* know the answer to. What had happened last night? He was hopelessly confused.

"Sorry, you can't shake me off. Are you alive in there? It's almost eleven o'clock. Should I be worried?"

He didn't know how to answer that yet. His head hurt most, but so did everything else below it. He reached up to touch his face, his eyes, various body parts. All still in order. But he still needed to buy some time to piece together the sequence of events.

Had the mushrooms been real?

Had he tried to climb last night?

How had he gotten back to the tent?

"I'm all good, thanks. I'll be out in a few minutes." The words pierced the back of his throat. Whatever had happened the night before, it felt like it had involved swallowing razor blades.

"OK, take your time. I have coffee and eggs out here, and it's a beautiful morning on the meadow."

A good time later, he unzipped the tent and peered out. He waited for his eyes to adjust to the light. The girl sat by the fire. A spitting pan of eggs sat on a small grill over the flames. She smiled warmly at him and poured them each a small cup of coffee. He stumbled out to sit on a rock next to the fire, and she handed him a cup.

He thanked her, not knowing where to look or what to say. She spoke first.

"I need to say this. I'm sorry for what I said last night about craving your parents' love. It's not my business, and I went too far, put you on the spot, and I feel terrible about it. I didn't know you lost your father. I hope you don't hate me."

"No, I'm sorry. I shouldn't have stormed off. They were good questions. We were just talking. I got angry because I've never had the guts to ask those questions myself."

The coffee burned his throat, and he winced. "It was too raw, too new for me. I do want to talk about it soon, find out things about myself. I need to. I loved listening to you all day yesterday. The path and the three minds. I learned a lot. I've never met anybody like you. I want to learn more if you don't mind walking more with me today."

She raised two thumbs and laughed. "Of course."

That was a relief at least.

There was a long silence then. He had so many questions.

"I had quite an adventure last night," he said. "After we argued, I started raging in the tent. I got so angry I stormed off into the forest. It was all pretty dumb. I got lost, I got cold, and I found some mushrooms I shouldn't have eaten.

At least I think I did. I got sick. I could have died out there. I had a trip, or a dream, or a vision, and it was very vivid. Somehow, I made it back to the tent, but God knows how." As he spoke, he reached into his sweater pocket, fumbling for proof that his story was true. He was relieved to find the tiny mushrooms there. It had happened after all.

"Do you remember what you dreamed about?"

"I do, but I'm not even sure the dream has ended yet, if that makes sense... It still feels alive, a part of this conversation, whenever I talk." He described the men at the crossroads, the chanting, his mother, and the colorful hummingbirds fluttering out of his head. "Everything I saw last night was vivid and deeply connected, almost perfect, and at the same time the hardest thing to describe. It was the wildest fantasy but somehow also the truest thing I've ever known."

She nodded. "I'm almost afraid to confess this, but I was there with you last night, in the forest. I hope you don't mind. I know you wanted to be alone. I thought maybe you needed me, and I definitely needed to be needed."

He was shocked. "You were with me? The whole time?"

"No, not the whole time. I didn't follow you in. I just found you on the ground in the forest, like a block of ice, coughing and sneezing. I could hear you from the meadow. You were delirious, rolling in the leaves, shouting to yourself. You didn't recognize me. I managed to walk you back to the camp. I lay you by the fire until you warmed up, and I boiled some ginger tea. After you'd warmed up, you started smiling and talking to yourself. I led you over to your tent and sat with you. You finally crashed in the end, very happy." She grinned. "Quite blissful, actually."

"I'm so sorry. I had no idea. Thank you for saving me. I really didn't deserve it, and you could have gotten hurt."

She leaned over and placed her finger on his lips. Her touch warmed him. "Actually, I meant what I said about needing you to need me. I needed to save somebody else. I know just how you felt. Nobody should ever be on a trip alone. It should only be a journey of joy, from a place of love to a place of deeper love, in the hands of a gentle guide."

Her words warmed him.

"You've tried eating mushrooms yourself?" he asked.

"I have. They can open up your mind in unexpected ways, so be prepared to see things differently for a few days. I tried almost everything in the past. But that was a long time ago, a different me. It wasn't a happy time. I don't look back."

He wanted to know. "Would you look back just a little for me? I don't even know who you are or anything about you. I just know you're wiser than I'll ever be, but how did you learn it all?"

It was the question he'd been desperate to ask since they'd met. She seemed perfect in every way to him. She seemed like a forest nymph or some other being from another world. She was like a guide sent to save him. But he also knew she was very real, and he feared knowing the truth. What if she turned out to be sad and lonely and lost like everybody else? He wanted her to be perfect, but he also needed to know she wasn't.

She sat there in sadness. "There's really no big story. I was fighting anxiety, and I was fighting depression, and they were winning, two against one." She attempted a smile.

"I don't even know the difference," he admitted.

Everything about her seemed more fragile as she talked. "Depression is being trapped in the present and the past; anxiety is being trapped in the future. And I wasn't just anxious; I could have handled that. I used to lie awake at night feeling anxious about feeling anxious. I had no ladder out, and I probably wouldn't have used it if I had one.

"I spent my best years with the worst people. It turns out it doesn't take long to find angry, violent people who need to own the people they think they love when that's who you're looking for. I gave everything, took everything, tried everything. I fell into a pattern. I would hold it all together for a few weeks, a functioning melancholic, but then I'd fall back into a hole again. I would spend weeks in bed and then go back out and spend weeks out on the streets.

"I wasted every chance to turn it around. I was a true addict, addicted to being addicted. I wanted my family and friends to hate me, and in the end the only person I lied to more than them was myself."

He had no idea what to say. This was far more truth than he'd bargained for. "I'm sorry. You don't need to tell me everything." It was a lie. He had to know now.

"I'm good. It's hard to start talking about it, but it's hard to stop when I've started. Don't worry. I promise there's a happy ending. But first I got kicked out of Stanford…"

"You were also at Stanford?"

"Born and raised on campus. Ma and Pa met there as students and became professors, a famous institution in their own right. My brother sailed through effortlessly. But on the day I got accepted, I knew I wouldn't make it through. The path was clear and straight in front of me, but I just couldn't walk it. It was too damn straight. I had to run away and find a big hole to fall into."

Her eyes glistened. "I got *really* screwed up. I was in deep, drowning quietly at the bottom of my hole. And then an angel reached in and fished me out and saved my sorry life."

"What happened?"

"My last remaining friend signed me up for a retreat, ten days of meditation and total silence. She drove me right to the door and walked me up to the desk. I'd been sober for a month, but I was just about to relapse, and she knew it. She didn't know she was saving my life that day though."

"The retreat helped, then. What was it like?"

"It looked like a school gym. They took away everything, all of our devices, even our books. They put me in a dorm with three other women, all silent. We were told not to look each other in the eyes. I didn't know their names or where they were from. They told us we'd start meditating that night and then every day for more than ten hours a day. We started at four thirty in the morning, and we ate small portions of vegan food."

"It sounds more like a prison."

"It felt like prison at first. I mean, that's even how they punish prisoners, isn't it? Solitary confinement? And at first it freaked me out, the idea of being so alone with myself, the person I hated most in the world. I tried to run before it even began, but the lady in charge talked me down, and I promised to try one hour at least. When it was time to meditate, they struck a gong, and we all filed into the hall, about a hundred of us, fifty men and fifty women. They divided us down the middle of the hall, seated on cushions, facing the front. They shared a few house rules and then played a recording with simple instructions for a few minutes, and we all started to meditate.

"We were just sitting in silence, paying attention to our breath, the air coming out of our nostrils, the sensation on our upper lip. It was all very simple, practical, and not religious at all. It immediately started to have a profound effect on me.

"From that first hour, I learned that I had almost no control over my mind, and my attention would spring like a grasshopper between past memories and anxiety about the future. Despite all my attempts to stay 'in the now.' The harder I tried, the worse it was. It was like somebody else was endlessly channel-flicking on a TV set I was trying to watch.

"They told us to focus on our normal breath through the nose, to keep going, stick to our practice with persistence. But after several hours, my brain ached. It was brutal. The hardest thing I've ever tried to do. After a few days, I slowly got the hang of it and learned to meditate using the rising and fading sensations in my body. I could observe my thoughts, but I still suffered setbacks and frustrations.

"To my surprise, the thing I feared the most, the total silence, was the easiest and most magical part of it all. That was eye-opening. With no need to talk or listen, I finally got to hear the sound of my own voice clearly and discover what I'd *really* been telling myself all of these years, second by second. I spent a lot of time thinking about where my inner voice had come from. I discovered that talk is cheap, and I'd wasted a great deal of energy telling stories to myself and others. And when I was free from all of those stories, all of that extra energy flowed through my body.

"By the tenth day, I was bursting with positive energy. I felt awake, excited about the future. I didn't fear a relapse. I didn't have all the answers, but I knew where to find them now: inside myself. I already knew everything I needed to know to live happily; I just needed to sit still enough to listen to myself.

"On the last day, we were allowed to talk to each other, and we made up for lost time. All the women hugged and shared their feelings, bonded by the shared experience. I'm still connected to many of them."

She looked up, and he could see the tears on her cheeks. "I'm sorry. This is the first time I've ever talked about all this."

He wanted to hold her, and he thought she wanted him to, but he didn't trust his instincts.

"Things became much clearer from that point on," she continued. "I carried on meditating twice a day. I started looking after my body, reading, thinking. All of my destructive habits slowly faded away. I traveled around the world, and my practice grew strong. I sat with teachers in India, Burma, Cambodia, and Thailand. I walked with pilgrims in Spain and France and the Middle East to understand what gives meaning to different people. And I learned to cultivate three new minds and make good choices.

"My family and friends all forgave me. I continue to make good choices, and those choices have led only to happiness. I've spent a lot of time thinking about a better way to live life. And when I meet a fellow traveler who looks lost, I try to walk and talk with them, to help them on their way."

They sat beside each other in the morning sun like two leading stage actors stripped of their makeup and costumes seeing each other for the first time.

She smiled. "Shall we walk and talk more? We still have a lot to cover. Or uncover, I should say. I'm learning from all of your questions too."

He nodded, and they began packing up their camp in silence. He felt she knew all the things he desperately wanted to learn, and his mind felt wide open. Whenever he listened to her, he wasn't thinking about his father, or the betrayal, or climbing the rock face.

Listening to her felt like imagining a future.

Choice of Plan

The meadow hummed with life as they made their way down the valley. The dirt track was wider and the grass shorter, so they could walk side by side.

They felt lighter now, more playful, sharing childhood memories and songs:

Don't walk in front of me…I may not follow
Don't walk behind me…I may not lead
Walk beside me…just be my friend

Then, as they sat for a drink by the stream, he took out his book and read out the principles from his notes:

> *The Path* – Take a path and walk it with a good mind and good choices.

> *The Grateful Mind* – Savor it all, every day, and always feel lucky.

> *The Compassionate Mind* – We must care and do more if possible, and it's always possible.

The Observing Mind – Neither chase nor avoid
things but accept them and be there in the middle.

"The path and the three minds all make sense, especially now I know about your life," the boy said. "But without the daily choices, it's all just theory, right?"

"Right. It's easy to sit around debating what makes a good or happy person. It's much harder to stand up and actually be one. I've learned that staying happy is much easier than I used to think it was. If I just make good choices most of the time, I'm almost always happy."

That sounded easy enough to him. He closed his eyes and tried to remember the nine choices on the triangle.

The girl was carefully building piles of stones by their feet, a pyramid of large rocks and a flatter pile of smaller pebbles next to it.

"Let's start where I start each day," she said, "with my first choice: a plan. Can you grab your camping pot, please?" She pointed to the tin pot clipped to his backpack.

He unclipped it and wiped it clean.

"Now please fill your pot with the stones from the pyramid," she said. "Fill it right up."

He did as she said. The pot gleamed in the sun, and the jagged rocks clanged as he dropped them in one by one until they reached the lip.

"Done!"

"Is it full now?"

"It's full, just about."

"OK, now please add in the other stones from the second pile. Again, fill it right up."

He scooped up the smaller pebbles, pouring them into the pot around the bigger rocks, shaking them down to the bottom, until the pot was full once again.

"OK," he said.

"Is it full now?"

"It is." He grinned. "It's getting heavy!"

"OK, now please add in sand from the stream. You know the drill. Fill 'er up."

He kneeled down beside the stream like a child at the beach and began pouring handfuls of dark, grainy sand into the pot. He scooped it a dozen times out of the water until it reached the brim of the pot.

"Is it full?" the girl asked.

"Well, I would say so, but my track record sucks. I'm sure you're going to show me otherwise." He laughed.

Finally, she asked him to fill the pot with water from the stream, which he did with his coffee mug until the pot was filled to the top.

He laughed again. "OK, I feel a valuable lesson is coming."

"And what lesson would that be?"

He took his time to work it out in his head. "I thought the pot was full each time, but it wasn't. And the only reason I could keep filling the pot was because I started with the big rocks, not the sand. If I'd started with the sand, there would have been no room for the smaller pebbles, let alone the big rocks. So, I guess it's teaching me to always start with the bigger ones, the most important things, and if I get all of those right first, I can still have a full pot, a full life."

She clapped theatrically. "Bravo! That's my first daily choice to make a plan. I choose a few big rocks each day and tackle them first. If you get the foundations right, you can do anything. I do it the night before, or before I get out of bed. Just a short list of the most important things I will do. I know the day will fill with sand if I don't plan for a few big rocks first. If I don't plan the important things, the world will find endless trivial things for me to do. If I make sure to get some big rocks into my pot, it's almost always going to be a good day."

"It makes sense, but I don't know if I could do it every day. I'm not great in the mornings. I take time to get going. Can I try it once a week at first?"

"Sorry, but you have to commit to this one every day, like brushing your teeth. You can plan in decades, think in years, but you must live each day at a time. You must become greedier and more protective about your time. It's not a new problem. As Seneca wrote two thousand years ago, 'We're tight-fisted with property and money, yet think too little of wasting time, the one thing about which we should all be the toughest misers.'"

It made sense to him. He dumped his pot out, rinsed it, and clipped it back onto his pack. He took out his notebook and wrote, "Choice of Plan – Pick a few big rocks each day and tackle them first."

He then tucked his notebook into his pack, and she helped him to his feet.

"One last question," he said. "What's your plan today? What are your big rocks?"

"Well, my first rock is to run through the first four or five choices with you by the time we make camp. My second rock is to finish a song I'm writing. And my third rock…well, that's my little secret for now. A girl's allowed to have some secrets."

He tried but failed to hide his joy. They would be camping together again that night. There would be another fire, more stories, and more opportunities for intimacy.

Choice of People

They left the path together to walk on the other side of the stream, side by side.

"Let's talk about the choice of people," the girl said. "First, I want you to stop and close your eyes for a moment. Try to think of a happy place with a spectacular sunset view. Somewhere where you can sit quietly and enjoy the final moments of the day."

After giving him some time to think, she said, "Have you found one?"

He smiled and nodded. He enjoyed how she turned everything into a game.

"OK, now imagine you're eighty years old, and you're sitting there with two or three extra chairs on either side of you. All of these wooden chairs face the sunset, and on each chair, you're going to seat somebody special from your life. They should be only the people you know now who you'll want to sit with you at the end. These are the people who always want the best for you, and you would do anything for them. One might be your partner, or a brother or sister or parent, but all of them are your friends."

"OK."

"I want you to sit with them in your mind for a while, looking out at the sunset, laughing and talking. You know you love them, and they love you, and they'll probably get along with each other too, even if they've never met. Enjoy the conversations in your mind. Those are your *forever friends*, the people who will change your life forever and will be there at the end, no matter how many decades or thousands of miles come between you."

He stood still, eyes shut, and tried to hide his disappointment as his mind rested on a row of empty chairs.

Nobody sat with him.

"We always need two types of people in our lives," the girl continued, "all the people we need to know for now, and the few people we will know forever. We also need to know who is in which group. Both are important for us as we walk through life, but we need to know the difference."

"I just see a lot of empty chairs," he admitted sadly.

"It doesn't matter if we have empty chairs right now because we're still young and we still have many years to find our forever friends. The important thing is to find a few people who truly want us to be happy and will do anything to help us succeed."

"I wish I had at least one chair filled," he sighed.

"Your empty chairs might mean you've been unlucky— maybe you didn't grow up on the right street or just never found your crowd. Or think about it the other way. Perhaps your empty chairs mean you're lucky—maybe you can take advantage of having a fresh start in finding your forever friends. That's an opportunity for a lot of fun. You have all that to look forward to. It all depends on your outlook."

"But what if I don't even need other people to be happy? I was an only child, and I'm an introvert, so I've always spent a lot of time alone. Sometimes I think life's simpler for a lone wolf. Nobody can stab you in the back, for a start."

There was an awkward pause, which the girl ignored.

"It sounds tempting, I know," she said, "and it can be good to be alone for a while. But it's not a good life plan. Humans are a social species, and we die earlier and unhappier when we try to disconnect from other people. We need other people to complete ourselves. We're physically wired to connect. Spending time with people releases important chemicals in our brains, and it's dangerous to cut yourself off from those chemicals."

"I get that, but do I really have to go out and choose all of these people? Can't I just let it happen naturally? Pick up friends randomly as I go along?"

"That sounds a lot easier, and most people do it that way, but leaving it all up to chance isn't a good plan. It's too important. One of the simplest ways to be happy is to choose happier friends. Whether you like it or not, people will judge you by the friends you have. More to the point, we're influenced by the people we associate with. If you don't choose your friends, your friends will choose you, and they could be the wrong people for you. They might not care about who you need to become. We get to choose that. We're not insects, and it's not the eighteenth century. We should take responsibility for who we spend time with."

He knew she was right, but he still had questions. "How do I choose the right partner and hold down a relationship? What do you look for?"

"Ha! If you're looking for personal expertise on romantic relationships, you're asking the wrong person. I'm hopeless, a total wrecking ball!"

He didn't believe her. She seemed perfect in every way.

"Actually, I'm so bad at it that I decided to learn from the experts," she said. "I read shelves of books by so-called gurus, but I didn't know who to believe. And then somebody told me to simply find a couple who've been happily together for a lifetime and just ask them. I knew only one couple like that, and they'd been sitting right in front of me the whole time: my own parents! After thirty years together, they still laugh at each other's jokes, support each other, and respect each other."

"Did you ask them their secret?"

"I drove straight over to see them, and when they opened their front door, I asked them outright what they'd been doing all of these years. Ma just hugged me and laughed and said, 'We thought you'd never ask.' I could have saved myself a lot of pain if I'd thought of asking them earlier."

"They're lucky to have found each other. You're lucky to have parents like that. What did they tell you?"

"A lot. First, they told me it's nothing to do with luck; it's just damn hard work. They said everybody tells stories about finding Mr. Right, being struck by Cupid's arrows, or experiencing chance encounters. But the truth is that love is a skill we can learn. They told me they used to fight like alley cats when they were starting out. Ma tore strips out of Pa, and he had no idea what she needed. He was clueless, so they fought, and the police used to get called out. They also spent years in counseling. I had no idea. They just stuck with it, and they became skillful and learned how to heal themselves together. Many of their friends and peers got divorced. They just got better.

"Second, they said love is a conversation. That's a simple one. It's about talking and listening and never leaving things unsaid. You can't heal what you can't hear.

"Next, they said love is a seesaw, and that's a good thing. You don't ride a seesaw just to sit there in perfect balance without moving. The whole point is to go up and down with someone you trust. They said they used to fight because things weren't balanced. One year, Pa's career was going really well, and he wasn't around much. The next year, Ma's career took off and so she had to travel a lot. And so on. After many years, they realized that balance only made sense over a lifetime. No single year was ever balanced.

"They also said love grows back fast when we stop causing each other pain. Apparently, my parents used to fight over the stupidest things and were always on the brink of ending things. He always left the toilet seat up. She always left all the lights on. One day, they just sat down and listed out everything that annoyed them, and they both promised to stop doing the little things that annoyed each other. The love grew back within a week. They'd listened to each other and made an effort. That's all they needed to know. They laugh about it now because they literally split up once over a pair of socks left on the floor.

"Also, love grows when we expect less. You can't expect your partner to change in all the specific ways you want them to. You *can* expect them to make an effort and to compromise, but you can't be precise about how and how fast. That's you thinking about what you need rather than putting what they need first. Happiness equals expectations minus reality.

"Finally, love grows when it comes first, even before kids. They told me how their biggest fights were about being parents. They had very different ideas about raising kids. I remember those times; it was like living in a war zone. They finally woke up one day and realized that their relationship was the most important thing to get right. If they stayed with each other and created a house full of laughter and love, the kids would turn out just fine. That apparently took all the pressure off, and they never looked back. And I guess it worked." She laughed. "Well, at least my brother turned out fairly normal!"

"Your parents sound amazing. Their list is great. But didn't they mention physical attraction?"

"It didn't make their list. I did ask about it. Pa called it an output not an input, and Ma just rolled her eyes and laughed. They always hugged a lot. I guess if everything else is working out, it just happens naturally."

"I can see how much you love them now, and how you still learn from them."

"I'm lucky that I grew up with happy parents. When I don't know what to do or think, I listen to my inner voice and I can hear them talking. Sometimes they disagree, but I hear them both. I think that's how it works. The way parents speak to their kids becomes an inner voice."

He felt a spark. He was afraid to listen to his own inner voice. He was trying to stay happy for her and not compare her house of laughter to the memories of his own parents' cold and loveless marriage. "It's a lot of hard work to make just one relationship work. Doesn't it scare you to think about that kind of commitment?"

"It terrifies me," she said. "Honestly, I'm a disaster. But at least I know why I'm so dangerous now. I talk way too much, and I don't really listen. I'm selfish. I love my freedom, and I don't need other people in the way they want to be needed."

"How do they want to be needed?"

"I have no idea. They just seem to want me to need them. When I don't, they get confused, and that's when things fall apart fast."

"That sounds tough."

"Not really, to be honest. I mean, it's true. I didn't need any of them. When people walk out on me, I'm always happy to be free again."

They walked in silence for a while. She then surprised him with a question.

"Do you regret not having a brother or sister?"

He thought hard about it. "My whole life I've always said no to that question. I've told people that I like having the space and the time to think. But now that my father's gone, I wish I had a sibling. I wish I had somebody to go back over everything with and piece it all together. I have all of these memories of my childhood, but I don't know how much of it is true. I can only ask my mother now, and she hates to talk about the past.

"A sibling is the longest relationship you can have. Longer than with your partner, and longer than with your parents. If I had one, and they'd shared all the same experiences as me, I think I'd want to hang out with them a lot. I mean, you don't get to choose your family, but if you have one, at least you get to choose how much time you spend with them."

After walking a bit farther along the stream, they agreed to look for a place to rest and eat. But he had one more question.

"Before we started talking about your parents, you said we need to find all the people we need to know for now as well as the few people we will know forever. How do you know who you need to know for now? Why do you even need them if they aren't going to stick around?"

"We will probably need to know hundreds, if not thousands, of people in a lifetime. They might know a special skill we have to learn or be part of an influential group or know someone important we need to know. We might know them well for a week or a month or a year of our lives, but then we might never see them again. We help them; they help us. It's a lightweight connection we make before moving on in our separate ways. These temporary connections add up over a lifetime and will help us in weird and unpredictable ways, especially when we're young and live in a vibrant city. It's how the world works."

"You're right, but I find meeting other people stressful. You make it sound so simple."

"Some people hate the game and others love it. I think life is easier and more fun when we stay open to meeting new people. It's how we grow. We observe tiny characteristics and mannerisms and try things out ourselves. We keep whatever works, and it becomes part of who we are.

"The important thing is not to confuse a friend for now with a friend forever. A friend for now might do a small favor to help you out, but a friend forever will drop everything to rescue you when you need it."

"I wonder why I haven't found a forever friend like that…"

"I'm not sure you've ever looked for one."

"Where would I look?"

"Start with knowing the kind of person you are and the type of people who give you energy instead of take it away. Most people tax your energy, but some people always leave you feeling recharged. That's because people are different likes. Some people like *things*, some people like *ideas*, some people like *experiences*, and some like *people*. Which one are you?"

"I like ideas most," he said quite confidently, "and it's true; the people I like the most also like talking about ideas."

"Is that right?"

"Yes, including you," he added, fishing for a smile.

She rewarded him with one. "So what's your principle going to be for this choice?"

After thinking about it for a while, he pulled out his notebook and wrote it down. Then he read aloud, "'Choice of People – Find the many people who are good for you now and the few people who want the best for you forever.'"

"Very nice, my friend."

"Your forever friend?"

She laughed. "One day, perhaps."

Choice of Meditation

They walked on in hungry silence for a while until they reached a large shady oak. They climbed up onto a ledge and sat on two flat rocks. Glistening with sweat, they gulped water from their flasks. The cicadas hummed in the nearby scrub, and they shared handfuls of trail mix. For every mouthful she took, he took five.

Then the rocks beneath them erupted with a terrifying sound.

Rattler!

The angry warning of a rattlesnake thundered right beneath them like a maraca piercing their ears. And then there it was, hissing at their feet. A triangular head poised, several feet of olive-brown scales writhing, and a black and white tail rattling.

The boy froze with ancient terror. He'd never been this close to a natural killer his whole life. He looked over at the girl, deafened, flabbergasted. Now he really was lost for words. The girl sat cross-legged. She was still. Her eyes were shut, and her lips were curled into a smile.

Was she insane? Wasn't she afraid?

"Are you *meditating*?" he hissed. He tried to make himself

heard over the incessant rattle, but he also didn't want to provoke the venomous snake.

She nodded, keeping her eyes closed, and spoke clearly over the sound. "Just close your eyes and sit perfectly still. Focus on your natural breath. Trust me on this. Just try to observe the air in your nostrils. Start now, and I'll tell you when to stop after our little friend has moved on."

His eyes widened in disbelief. The snake moved closer, just a foot from his toes. The rattle was deafening. Then, to his surprise, he managed to close his eyes. He did as she instructed and observed the breath on his upper lip, noting all the frantic thoughts hurtling through his mind. He thought he felt the snake glide across his left foot now. Why not? he thought. The night before, he'd planned to die on a hallucinogenic climb. Why not keep things simple and get bitten by a rattler?

They sat still for the longest and most heart-pounding minute of his life, then the noise stopped. His ears rang in the silence, and the hum of the cicadas slowly returned to the meadow. He tried to keep focusing on the air in his nostrils, desperately trying to note every manic thought and come back to the breath. He sneaked a few peeks and saw her sitting in happy stillness. He felt like a character in a fairy tale, longing to be released from a spell.

Finally, she released him.

"I think the percussion section went to practice somewhere else!" she joked.

"That was insane! Actually, no. *You're* insane! I can't believe you meditated your way through that."

They both burst out laughing, unable to stop, clinging to the rocky ledge for balance.

"I know," she said. "I'm sorry that your first meditation session was to save your life, but it was kinda fun, right?" She laughed again.

"I was terrified. How did you expect me to focus on my breath with a set of venomous fangs pointing at my crotch? Seriously, though, were you really feeling calm just now? Weren't you panicking? Is that how they trained you at meditation school?"

"I've never tried to meditate while in physical danger before, but, yes, I felt pretty calm. I've felt pretty calm ever since I started practicing meditation. It helps me see things as they are, at their roots. It puts stillness and space between my thoughts and my reactions, and it helps me make better decisions in the real world. It strengthens my observing mind, which helps even when I'm not meditating. I can now properly show you how it works if you like. It doesn't take long to learn."

"I'll pass for now," he said. "Maybe later. I don't think I'm cut out for sitting still. It doesn't make me calmer; it makes me anxious. I don't really believe in it."

"It's not something you need to believe in. It's just a technique to try, and it either works or it doesn't. Preferably without a rattlesnake. Come on! Try it once with me, then you can decide if it's for you."

He relented, and she took his hand, leading him down to the shady base of another tree.

She showed him how to sit comfortably, legs crossed, back straight, hands laid gently in his lap. He struggled with the upright posture, so she helped him prop his back against the tree, comfortable but alert.

They closed their eyes and sat in silence.

She showed him how to focus on his breath, his natural breath, flowing in and out of his nose. She directed him to a tiny area of skin below his nostrils as the breath came gently in and went gently out. He felt his breath touch his skin and the hairs on his upper lip. It was sometimes cool, sometimes warm, like a tiny electric pulse.

His mind wandered every few seconds, as she had warned him. His attention jumped between past memories and future anxieties. He found it impossible to stop the endless flow of random thoughts and ideas. When he sighed in frustration, she reminded him to note the thoughts as they arose and faded rather than judge them or cling to them. Just observe. When he felt himself getting too attached to a persistent thought, she gave him four words to help him move on and return home: *back to the breath.*

His mind sometimes fixed on the soreness in his legs and the discomfort of his back pressing against the craggy tree. She told him to note these distracting sensations and use them to keep his attention on the impermanence of the world. He watched them rise and gently fade away.

They sat like this for almost an hour as if their straight spines were rooted to the tree. Then finally she invited him to open his eyes and stretch his legs.

He smiled and nodded, keeping his eyes closed for another minute to savor several more breaths under the tree. Then he stood up and quietly paced around the tree a while. He was excited to talk more about it. He had questions but didn't want to break the silence. She spoke first.

"You were smiling a lot for your first meditation.

How did you find it?"

"It was energizing, not calming. Not at all how I'd imagined it. How does it work? What just happened?"

"You're right. It is energizing. I can tell you how it works for me, on many levels. First, since I'm sitting still, I can hear myself enough to study my own mind. Instead of looking out from my mind, I look inward and can observe it. I see how I crave the past and fear the future, and I see how I can't control my own thoughts.

"Second, when I note my thoughts and sensations rising and falling, I can see the truth about the world, that everything comes and goes, that nothing is permanent. Why get worked up about it? All bad things will come to an end.

"Third, when I focus on my breath and the sensations in my body, I'm reminded that these are knowable truths, and they are always available to me wherever I am, whenever I need to find the truth.

"Fourth, when I meditate, I practice putting a short space between my thoughts and my reactions to my thoughts, and this prevents me from getting hijacked by them. This reminds me that I am not my thoughts. My thoughts often think themselves into being, but I don't need to cling to them.

"Finally, when I meditate, I stop wanting, which makes me see more clearly and make better decisions, even long after I've stopped meditating."

He felt like an explorer discovering a new land. There were still so many questions. "When we can control our minds like this, is that mindfulness?"

"We never fully control our minds, but, yes, mindfulness is an awareness that arises when we pay attention in the present moment and without judgment. It's about living here in the now, never longing for the next place, never expecting it to be more fulfilling than this moment."

"And do you need to meditate every day? Or only when you need to recharge?"

"Daily practice is far better, even if it's only twenty minutes each morning. I think of it as part of my daily performance. Think about it. We wake up every day, and we all go out to perform in a way. We pick up our instrument, walk out onto the stage under the lights, and start playing for the world. We give it our best, strumming and singing for others. So does it make sense to walk straight out onto the stage without first tuning up your instrument and practicing a bit? Isn't it worth spending time alone to tune things just right and play a few chords and a few scales just for yourself?" She then played air guitar, making him laugh.

"And what about enlightenment? Or nirvana? Does meditation ever bring you to a state of bliss?"

"I can share a personal story about that. On the fourth day of my first retreat, we were finally given permission to move beyond our focus on the upper lip. They invited us to explore all the other sensations around our bodies. Within seconds of mentally scanning my body for sensations, I began to feel overwhelmed by endless waves of bliss. My body pulsed and radiated, and an irrepressible grin spread across my face. It felt like I was glowing, and I opened my eyes to see if anybody else had noticed. Of course, everybody was still locked in meditation, but I was overwhelmed. I thought I'd found enlightenment in just four days of my first retreat."

"That sounds awesome."

"I thought so."

"What happened?"

"I felt proud, special, and saved. I wanted to share it with somebody, but we had six more days of silence to go, so I decided to approach the monk during the lunchtime break. We were allowed to consult him each day on matters relating to our practice. I told him about my experience and my joy and thanked him for his role in my miracle. He listened at first but then cut me off sternly. 'Please get back to your meditation now and work harder to avoid attachment to your cravings and desires,' he said, and he dismissed me with a wave of his hand."

"What did you do?"

"That was it. That was my personal moment of meditation nirvana. A self-induced hour of intense bliss was almost certainly a flight of my own ego. I was craving bliss, trying to 'win' and cling to something that would make me feel special. I knew at that moment I was in the right place if I wanted to change and learn how to free my mind of craving and aversion.

"I'm afraid enlightenment isn't a very helpful concept here. You will have good days and bad days, and your practice should strengthen steadily over the years, but nobody is handing out black belts or trophies to meditators. If nirvana does exist, it's not a useful goal."

"If I start meditating regularly, or go to a retreat, does that make me a Buddhist?"

"Absolutely not. You can meditate or go on a retreat without knowing anything about any of the types of Buddhism. Most of the people I've met at retreats would not call themselves Buddhists. Some follow other religions; some have no religion. And it's not all about money because at many retreats you pay only what you can afford or choose to pay. The technique I learned is supposed to be a pure form of the Buddha's teaching practiced twenty-six centuries ago in India, but you can practice it without following rituals or believing in reincarnation, for instance."

He felt relieved.

"If you're interested in exploring Buddhist meditation," she continued, "there's an old saying about the three main traditions, Zen, Tibetan, and Vipassana, which captures their differences. According to the saying, Zen is for the poets, Tibetan is for the artists, and Vipassana is for the psychologists and scientists. It's a simplification, but it holds some truth. Zen Buddhists often meditate using cryptic lines of poetry called kōans. Tibetan meditation draws on visual imagery. Vipassana, however, is rooted in the mechanics of the mind and how the brain and body connect and influence each other. It sometimes feels like a branch of neuroscience. That's the one I know best. It's what I showed you today. *Vipassana* means 'to see things as they really are.' It's really a meditation technique that gets straight down to the root causes of things, and it doesn't use verbalization or visualization tools."

"Root causes and cravings? You make it sound like therapy."

"That's a useful comparison. It's not therapy, but I know many people who have beaten their addictions and demons far more effectively through meditation than through medication. It's as if the love and energy of strong meditation melts the cravings away and the positive new habit replaces the old ones. They say the best way to break bad habits is to upgrade your addictions. Vipassana especially can go deeper than other types of meditation. It tackles the deep roots of the mind to ensure the whole tree can be healthy long into the future."

"But how can it cure addictions?"

"For a start, a ten-day retreat forces you to abstain from many things, which helps get you started. No devices, no alcohol, no meat, no dairy, no cigarettes, no substances, no sexual intimacy. It's a total cold-turkey detox."

"Wow."

"Yes, but perhaps most important is there's something very valuable about the way you learn to dispassionately observe a bad habit, or even an addiction, during meditation. You might say there are three ways to respond to a demon: run, fight, or just let it in and observe it. When we choose the third option, we often steal its power."

"Did that happen to you?"

"Yes. That's how I quit smoking. I was addicted. I smoked a pack of cigarettes a day, sometimes more. I hated it, but I couldn't quit. The nicotine craving during my first retreat was unbearable. I used to stare out at the moon from my dormitory window, crying and shaking. I stuck it out, and I thought I'd kicked nicotine for good, but I found myself smoking again when I was triggered by the memory of an old feud a week later. A few sticks a day at first, then I was right back to where I started."

"I guess you were able to quit again?"

"Luckily, my meditation practice was still going strong. The more I sat with the habit and invited it in and observed it, the weaker the attachment became. Whenever I felt the craving, I would take a cigarette out, hold it up, inspect it, crumble it, and even laugh at it. And then one day, I didn't even feel the urge. I haven't smoked since or even wanted to. It's like I stole its power with my observing mind."

"Whoa…. Observer Girl, my new superhero!"

She laughed. "That's me!" She thrust an arm toward the sky.

The boy sat for a while and drained the last swig from his flask. "I think I get it now, but there's still one thing that doesn't make sense. If meditation is so useful and available to us, why doesn't everyone do it? It's like a superpower that most people don't even know they have."

"I agree. The French mathematician Pascal said it best: 'All of humanity's problems stem from man's inability to sit quietly in a room alone.' People don't make big changes easily. They fear the unknown, and they make jokes about what they don't understand. They underestimate their ability to break old habit and make new ones. I often hear people say that they get the same benefits from exercise — running or cycling or swimming — but it's not the same benefit. Running is great for the body and probably good for the mind, but people often run as a way to *avoid* their root problems. I don't blame them. Facing our demons is terrifying."

He bowed his head and thanked her for being his first meditation teacher.

She returned the gesture. "When the student is ready, the teacher always appears."

"I'll start a daily practice. It can only help. And now I know what to write in my notes." Once he had it written down, he read it out to her. "'Choice of Meditation – Sit still in the moment and observe each passing thought and sensation without judgment.'"

"That's beautiful. I can't wait to read your book one day."

"*Our* book, you mean."

They laughed, refilled their flasks and walked back out onto the path.

Choice of Body

They walked in the afternoon sun and enjoyed the silence for over an hour until they reached the foot of a small but steep hillside.

"Are you up for a little challenge?" the girl said. She dropped her pack to the ground and pointed up the rocky slope. "Let's get our hearts pumping a little."

"Sure," the boy said, even though he was already sweaty from walking, "I didn't take you for a runner."

He took off his pack and rested it next to hers. He was about to suggest they drink some water first, but she was already gone. She darted nimbly between the stones up toward the peak above them. She ran well. He took a few quick gulps of water and gave chase.

It felt good to run again. His legs pumped as he dug his toes into the side of the hill and powered himself up behind her. He felt his heart pounding in his chest. He also felt a slight stitch in his ribs, but it was a good pain to have. He sucked the air down into his lungs, smiling as he exhaled. He was even with her for a moment before easily passing with a few hundred yards to go.

When he reached the top, he looked down. He wiped the

sweat from his brow and placed his hands on his hips. She ran steadily toward him, and he cheered her on as she reached the summit. She laughed as she stumbled the final steps to the top. Exhausted, she thrust out her arms to break her fall. He caught her, and they held each other tightly, chests pounding together. She was even lighter than he expected, and he felt strong holding her. She was breathing too hard to speak, but it didn't matter because they couldn't control their laughter.

She pulled her wet face from his shoulder and looked up at him, smiling. "It feels good, right?"

"It certainly does."

Their hearts slowly settled down.

"I should probably warn you," she said, still gripping his arms. "I will never be the one to let go of a hug first."

"Ah! Oh, uh, sorry!" He pulled back and broke away from her.

She stood in front of him, bright teeth flashing. He felt confused and awkward, just like when they first met at the crossroads. He could still feel her warmth across his chest, and he thought briefly about the early days with Claudia, the good days.

"Shall we sit here and talk about the choice of body?" she asked.

He'd always kept himself fit. He'd even researched diets and studied physiology. He was interested to hear what she had to say about the subject, but she started with a curveball.

"I've been talking all day, and I'm still out of breath, so why don't you start this time?"

"What?" he asked. "Really?"

"You look like you take care of yourself. Our body is the

only place we have to live, so we need to start looking after it as early as possible. What's *your* secret routine? It's my turn to learn something."

He blushed and instinctively tightened his abs and flexed his triceps. "I'll need to think a bit. After all the talk about meditation, I thought you were going to explain how the mind and body are connected."

"I wasn't but tell me more. I don't think anyone knows much about that yet, do they?"

"Actually, we know a lot about it now, even at the chemical level. Running up that hill just boosted our neurotransmitters, including serotonin, dopamine, and noradrenaline. It almost certainly helped us focus our attention and activated our hippocampus. And the effects can be long-lasting, especially if we exercise regularly. We know that when our bodies get too run down, we get more anxious. And when our anxiety levels go down, our energy levels go up. But you probably knew all of that already."

"I didn't, but I do now. Thank you. I get overwhelmed by all the different nutrition and health studies, so I need to follow a very simple routine. I always think about how it would be easier to be a cavewoman, with fewer choices. That's our biggest problem: abundance. There is too much cheap, bad food on the supermarket shelves. Too much health news. Too many diets, fitness plans, supplements, and gadgets. Supersized portions. I bet Cavewoman Clara was healthier and less stressed about her choices than most of us today. Maybe that should be our guide: What would Cavewoman Clara do?"

He laughed. "OK, let's start there then. Caveman Chris

and Cavewoman Clara. Let's call them the Caveys. How can we live more like them? Not *exactly* like them, because that would get boring fast, but *more* like them. What would they eat?"

"They'd eat a lot less for sure, so that would be a good thing. Probably fewer meals and smaller portions. They were hunter-gatherers, so they'd probably snack lightly throughout the day. Fruits, vegetables, nuts, seeds, fish, eggs, some meat if you could catch it. Sometimes they'd find nothing, so they'd have to fast a little. I think I could handle that."

"Absolutely. If you keep good food like that in your kitchen, you will eat good food. I'm fine until I find myself near an easy source of bad food. Most health problems are problems of abundance. Obesity, blocked arteries, diabetes, high cholesterol, alcoholism. We become what we eat. Just eating real food would be a good place to start for most people today. A lot of what people buy isn't even food; it's chemicals, sugar, packaging. If you're eating real food, then almost everything's fine in moderation. We often buy junk food and tell ourselves it's a reward for some small achievement, like getting to the end of the day. But junk food isn't a reward; it's a punishment."

"Agreed. What about exercise then? Would the Caveys have to work out?"

"Well, they wouldn't have any equipment or gym memberships or tracking devices. And I don't think they'd feel the need to run marathons or swim a few miles on a Sunday morning. I think they'd have to keep moving around a lot and would break a sweat by chasing wild boars, spearfishing, and even just by gathering plants."

"And don't forget a fair bit of wrestling and some cave sex," the girl said with a straight face.

"OK, so let's just say we'd need to keep moving around and break a sweat at least once a day, but we'd have no need for triathlon training."

"Deal. I can handle that too! What about sleep then?"

"Good point. I forgot about that. The three most important choices are food, exercise, and sleep. Sleep is a great investment in the energy we need to be effective the following day. I think the Caveys would enjoy a solid eight hours a night, maybe longer. They'd have no artificial lights, no screens, no commutes. That's enough to let the body repair itself. They'd wake up refreshed and well-rested."

"And they'd need all of that sleep to dream properly," the girl added. "Think about how important dreams would have been for the Caveys, for creating stories to make sense of the world around them. They had no movies or books to make sense of it all, so it's no wonder early human beings evolved the power to dream."

"You're right. I don't always remember my dreams, but I'm sure they're still important. I think of them as the stories we haven't had time or permission to play out during the day. It's like we get to file away every memory in the right folders of our minds so we can start fresh again, reborn."

"I think we just solved the question of choice of body together. It's very simple. Just do what the Caveys did. But how are you going to write it in your notebook?"

He looked out over the treetops, racking his brain until he had it right. "I was thinking maybe eat less, mainly plants; break sweat; and sleep."

She repeated it a few times. "It's good, but something's missing. And I think I know what it is. Have you ever practiced yoga? If you like meditation, you're going to love yoga."

He hadn't. Like meditation, he'd always found it too intimidating and odd.

"This is the perfect place to initiate a new yogi," she said, springing up and spinning around, gesturing at tree canopy beneath them.

He sighed. "Do I have a choice?"

She took his hand again and walked him over to a flat ledge covered with a carpet of soft moss.

They stood straight, side by side, looking out over the tree line.

She breathed in deeply, stretched her arms out far, reaching up to the sky, holding her pose at the top.

He followed her movements, her breathing, and the gentle instructions she gave.

She taught him how to arrive gently into each posture and seek the edges, with deep breaths, like a surfer on a wave.

Each shape he learned was new, but he felt he had always known them: mountain pose, downward dog, warrior, plank, child, tree.

She showed him how to control his breath through his nose from his diaphragm, narrowing his throat to make a deep ocean sound.

She helped him find firmness, rooted to the mossy ledge but always relaxed.

They practiced focusing their gaze, eyes and mind locked together and anchored on a single point of energy.

She brought him out of the final pose gently, and they lay on their backs in silence, just with their breath.

He spoke first. "That was intense. I feel exhausted, body and mind, but charged with energy. Thank you. It was quite a workout!"

"In yoga, we sometimes call it a 'work in'…" She grinned. "I'm glad you found it tough. That means you needed it. The first few times are always the most intense. You're scrubbing the floors of your body and mind after years of neglect, shining a light into your dustiest corners. The poses where you have the most resistance are actually the ones that are going to bring the greatest reward."

"But what's the reward?"

"Yoga builds resistance. We bend so we don't break. We inhale the future; we exhale the past."

He nodded, taking it all in, his body all stretched out and still pulsating.

"We should head down the hill now," she said. "We need to walk on and make camp before sunset. But before we do, I think you now have the line finalized for your notebook, right?"

"Uh, I think I do." He smiled as he wrote it down. He then read aloud, "'Choice of Body – Eat less, mainly plants; sweat; stretch; and sleep.'"

Choice of Nature

They clambered back down the hill, tasting the cool evening air. They grabbed their packs and walked on until the sky melted into gold across the craggy skyline.

When it was time to make camp, the boy built a large fire with logs from the nearby woods and prepared a vegetable stew. As he did this, the girl meditated beneath a willow tree. They ate without words and then she washed everything up in the stream while he gazed deeply into the fire. It had been a long day, and there was a lot to think about.

"Are you ready for the final talk of the day?" the girl asked finally. "We covered the choices of plan, people, meditation, and body. The next is the choice of nature."

"I'm ready, and I think it's going to be my favorite."

"Why is that?"

"I always feel happier and healthier in places like this. It's simpler and quieter, and I can taste the air. It brings us closer to how those Caveys used to live thousands of years ago. Time outside in nature is just good for us. The higher levels of oxygen in the brain boost serotonin, and vitamin D lifts our mood and lowers our blood pressure and stress hormone levels."

"I didn't know that, but I'm not surprised. For me, time in nature is all about getting closer to the truth of things. The more we observe and connect to nature—animals, trees, the sea, the stars, the mountains—the more the truth reveals itself. We get to see through all the stories and delusions we weave for ourselves, and we can finally grasp who we really are. Through nature, we can smell, taste, touch, and know real things. Einstein said, 'Look deep into nature and then you will understand everything better.' We may never know the absolute truth, but we will grow happier the closer we are to it."

He was inspired by her excitement, but he needed something more concrete. It all felt too theoretical. "Those are big claims. What do you mean by the truth? How exactly does nature reveal it?"

She stoked the fire with a giant stick. "I can tell you how it reveals its truth to me, if you like."

"Sure."

"They once asked physicist Richard Feynman to sum up all scientific knowledge in one sentence. He answered simply: 'Everything is made of atoms.' He also said you can recognize the truth by its beauty and simplicity. The more I thought about Feynman's words, the more they inspired me. I started to get up close to nature and spend more time with whatever I could find that was beautiful and simple. I would walk out and find something and then study all the science behind it. The math, the patterns, the atomic building blocks. How it connected up with everything else, across time and species. I once found the most simple and beautiful thing I could find: a single petal of a flower. I spent a week trying to understand it. That's where I looked for the truth and stayed rooted in what is real."

They looked into the fire, feeling its warmth on their faces, logs spitting and crackling.

"So nature is like a door to the truth for you?" the boy asked.

"Almost. I think of nature and science as my two keys to unlock the door to the truth. I stick to the classic natural sciences: physics, chemistry, astronomy, earth sciences, botany, zoology. They provide the facts but also a whole way of thinking, a system of patterns and mysteries to solve. I realized I'd wasted so many years at school chasing grades and not really listening to the important lessons of science, and so I had a lot of catching up to do. I read voraciously. We all have an instinct for seeking the truth, uncovering what is real, but somehow we've created a world for ourselves where the truth is hidden deep away behind our stories, screens, and machines. It's as if we're trying to hide from it. I discovered it was all there waiting for me, in books and out here in nature. All the best and most beautiful and truest stories are waiting to be discovered."

"What kinds of stories?"

"Nature's stories are everywhere. How many do you want to hear?"

"We have a campfire, and I have all night." He grinned. "Start telling some, and I'll tell you when to stop."

"OK, you asked for it. Do you remember all the cicadas singing across the meadow today? I can tell you a beautiful story about cicadas and mathematical patterns. There are around fifteen hundred known species of cicadas. Most appear each summer, but some are called *Magicicada*. They grow slowly, underground, before surfacing en masse at either thirteen- or seventeen-year intervals, when the ground temperature hits a certain level. The nymphs finally emerge as adults, mate, lay their eggs, and die, all within the same few weeks of every thirteenth or seventeenth year. They have the longest lifecycles known for insects, and not one but three species do this, always together. Their ability to emerge in swarms by the million within a matter of hours, after spending more than a dozen years underground as silent, lonely children, is without parallel in the animal kingdom."

"That's insane." He sketched by the firelight as she talked.

"There's more. Why do they emerge in thirteen- and seventeen-year intervals? Why thirteen and not twelve or fourteen years? Well, the fact that thirteen and seventeen are both prime numbers is no coincidence. It creates two different survival advantages. First, a prime-numbered lifespan means that predators cannot match their lifecycles to the availability of cicada prey. For instance, if the cicadas had even-numbered lifespans instead of larger prime numbers, a predator with a two-year lifecycle, like a cicada killer wasp or a bird, could feast on cicadas every few generations.

"The second advantage is that prime number lifespans ensure fewer overlaps between different cicada species, so they very rarely swarm together to fight for the same food supply or crossbreed. In fact, a thirteen-year cycle and a seventeen-year cycle will only coincide once every two hundred twenty-one years, which is thirteen multiplied by seventeen."

"That's so beautiful," the boy said. "I'll never listen to a cicada song in the same way again. Keep going. What's next?"

"Do you know how acacia trees on the African savanna protect themselves from hungry giraffes? Or how the giraffes respond? Within minutes of giraffes starting to feed on umbrella thorn acacias, the trees start pumping toxic substances into their leaves to protect themselves. This forces the giraffes to move off and find new trees to munch on. But the acacia trees don't just pump toxins into their leaves; they also give off a warning to neighboring acacias. Those trees also protect themselves using the toxins, so the giraffes usually have to move on more than a hundred yards away. But the giraffes are also smart. They head upwind to eat the acacias that haven't been alerted yet because they appear to know that the scented message travels only downwind on the breeze."

"Smart trees, smart giraffes!"

"Yes, but not as smart as my hummingbird!" She proudly displayed her colorful wrist tattoo. "Did you know her brain is proportionally larger than any other bird's and almost twice the relative size of a human brain? She remembers every flower she ever visited, even on her long migration routes, and she somehow knows when it's time to return for fresh nectar. She drinks nectar but won't drink any that's less than ten percent sugar. She also recognizes different humans. Her eyes process ultraviolet light, which means she can see colors we can't, and at an early age she learned to prefer red flowers."

"Clever bird! What about bees? My uncle had beehives and used to drip the honey fresh off the comb for me. He'd tell stories about how the bees dance to signal where the best nectar is. I was convinced he was making it all up."

"Your uncle's stories were true. Bee talk is ingenious. Their figure-eight movement is called a waggle dance. The direction the bee moves in relation to the hive and the sun points to their target destination, and the duration of the waggle signifies the distance. But get this. The wagglers can adjust the angles of their dances to match the changing direction of the sun over time so the other bees can still find the food source even though its angle relative to the sun has changed."

"Whoa!"

"And did you know that honeybees team up to fend off their arch enemy, the giant hornet? Giant hornets are massive and lethal. They raid bees' nests, decapitate every bee in sight, and take the bodies back to feed their young. They also secrete a hormone to attract other hornets to attack en masse and destroy the entire colony. A bee's stinger can't penetrate a hornet's thick exoskeleton, so they're defenseless on their own."

"So how do they fight back?"

"By thermo-balling. They set up a defense squad at the entrance of the nest. Up to five hundred bees then mob the hornet, wrapping it up in a giant bee ball. They then flap their wings to create heat, raising the temperature enough to kill the huge attacker. There's even a variation of this behavior for a species called the oriental hornet which can withstand this higher heat. Cyprian honeybees have learned to suffocate these hornets by crushing their abdomens rather than overheating them. Game over!"

They both cheered for the bees.

"Zeus would be proud of them!" the boy said.

"Why Zeus?"

"It's the only story from Aesop's fables I still remember. Zeus loved the bee's honey so much he granted her any wish. She hated the fact that humans stole her honey, so she requested a vicious sting to attack them with. The bee's selfish choice made the god angry, so he granted her wish but also made it fatal for the bee to sting anybody. Her sting would remain in the wound and she would die. A real Greek tragedy. And that's how the bee got its sting."

She applauded with delight. "It just shows that you should never ignore insects," the girl said. "They say that all life on Earth would end within fifty years if every insect were to disappear. Yet, if all human beings disappeared, all forms of life would flourish again within fifty years."

She carried on sharing campfire stories, species by species, pattern by pattern. She explained the Fibonacci sequence behind spiral shells and how fractal shapes in trees and river systems have influenced architecture and industrial design.

"More than two thousand years ago," she continued, "Euclid said, 'The laws of nature are but the mathematical thoughts of God,' and I believe everybody can enjoy the same beautiful truths, whether they believe in a god, natural selection, or both."

"OK, you've convinced me that nature has the best stories. I need to spend more time out here studying these patterns for myself. There's nothing I'd enjoy more, to be honest, and it would be good for me. But I still believe humans are more interesting and important to understand than animals and plants. People are more complex."

"Maybe. And maybe not. Most people have no idea how complex the natural world is. They don't know what to look for. They literally can't see the forest for the trees. In fact, trees are a great example." She waved a hand toward the forest.

"How so?"

"We're only just beginning to learn how sophisticated tree communication is, how social they truly are. They call it the 'Wood Wide Web.' Trees help other trees through their root systems, either directly by intertwining their roots or indirectly by growing giant networks of fungi around the roots as a nervous system connecting individual trees. In fact, the largest living thing on Earth is a primitive honey fungus as large as a city block, hiding under the forest floor in the Blue Mountains in Oregon."

"Wow."

"Trees can even tell their own roots from those of their relatives. They build communities and work together, just as humans do. A single tree is exposed to the elements, to wind and weather, but a forest develops its own protective local climate. It stores water, balances temperature, and nurtures humidity. Trees grow more safely to an older age in denser forests where there are fewer large gaps in the tree canopy. Gaps allow storms inside, which can uproot more trees. Forests stick together and support sick individual trees until they recover. Trees care for each other, reciprocate. You see, trees have societies too, living in slow motion alongside ours, playing out over hundreds and thousands of years."

"I really had no idea. I just see trees and take them for granted. I didn't realize all of this happens beneath the surface. It's beautiful when you discover it."

"Most people never do, but these stories are always around for those who look. Nature is our wisest and most patient teacher. When you know trees, you know persistence, interconnection, and community. When you start to think of nature as your patient teacher, every sound and smell outdoors becomes a gift just for you."

"Your stories are beautiful," the boy said quietly. "I'd like to live much closer to nature so I can be closer to it every day." He really meant it.

"You should. I'm always far happier in the company of people who live by the sea or in the mountains. They seem more at ease with their place in the universe. They've seen nature give lessons and take lives, and they've learned to respect it. When I get trapped inside a concrete jungle for weeks at a time, I get sick."

"Physically sick?"

"Yes. Deep down I'm just a primate. Have you seen what happens to animals in cages? Zoos are for people, not animals. Animals suffer from 'zoochosis' in captivity. They develop nervous tics and repetitive behavior such as pacing, figure-eight swimming, hair plucking, and even eating their own vomit." As she spoke, the flames flickered in her eyes. "I become like an animal in the zoo when I get trapped in a city for too long. I get human zoochosis. I need to run back to nature to connect with the truth."

She looked over and caught him studying her, his hand still moving over the page as he watched. "Are you drawing me?"

"I might be."

"Stop it! Don't!"

"Too late. I'm already stealing your soul."

"Throw it in the fire now."

"Stop moving your lips."

They continued talking until the flames died down and

just the embers glowed at their feet. Eventually he finished drawing and proposed a line: Choice of Nature – Connect with nature to keep rooted and closer to the truth. She told him she loved it, but she could see he still wasn't convinced.

"What's wrong?" she asked.

"Nothing, really. I just don't feel that much closer to the truth. I'm searching for answers up here in the mountains, so I want to get right down to the truth. Everything you're teaching me is helpful, but what if at the end of all of this I just have a notebook full of sentences and sketches? What if I do everything you say—take a path and walk it with a good mind and good choices—and I still feel lost?"

"What kind of truth are you looking for?"

"I don't know. I guess something deeper. Something that connects *me* to the world in a meaningful way."

She jumped up in the darkness and pulled him up to his feet. "I think you might be very close to finding what you're looking for. Remember how I didn't tell you about the third rock surprise on my plan today? Come with me. It's time to show you something you've never seen before."

The Truth

The girl led him across the meadow toward the edge of the forest, and together they stepped inside. His eyes were still adjusting to the darkness after the light of the campfire, so he had to rely on her for directions. He clutched her hand tightly. The trees were thick here, but they almost seemed to part for her as she walked, and the moon lit up a silver tunnel ahead of them, inviting them in deeper.

"OK, close your eyes now," she whispered. "I've got a surprise for you."

He closed his eyes tightly, shuffling forward blindly until he felt rocks beneath his feet. He felt steam on his face, and there was a gentle and familiar smell, like chemicals from a school lab. The fumes filled his nostrils, and he started sneezing uncontrollably. They both laughed. She then told him to open his eyes.

He opened his eyes and blinked in disbelief. They were standing on the rocky edge of a large bubbling pool of water. Steam rose from it into the night air. The surface glimmered like quicksilver in the moonlight. A black wall of trees circled the hot spring, and every few seconds a firefly flashed above their heads. Above them were countless stars. It was the most beautiful place he'd ever seen.

"Do you like my natural hot tub?" she asked. "I found it last year. I just had to show it to someone."

He nodded, speechless.

"Good. Because the last one into the water is a loser!" She kicked off her shoes and ripped open the zipper on her jacket.

Seconds later, they were splashing in the hot spring, laughing and ducking down to feel for the cracks where the hot water entered the pool. They lunged at fireflies, and their screams echoed around the glade.

He swam to the end of the pool on his own and dove underwater. He rolled onto his back, eyes open, and stared up through the water at the moonlight flickering upon the surface. He smiled. He had never been happier in his life.

Resurfacing, he gazed up at the stars.

The girl swam up beside him and whispered, "You love the night sky."

"I used to have a telescope in my bedroom and NASA posters on my wall. I spent years trying to find new planets. I was a bit of a space nerd." He laughed. "OK, I confess. I was a huge space nerd."

"OK, drop some space knowledge on me then," she challenged.

"Me? Now? I can't even remember. It was a long time ago."

"Sure you can. Nerds never forget."

"Ha! You're such a little kid. OK. Do you like big numbers? All kids love big numbers. Each galaxy contains hundreds of billions of stars, and there are probably more than a hundred billion galaxies in the universe. The most common stars are red dwarfs, which are less than half the size and mass of our sun. But they burn their fuel much more slowly, so they will live longer, more than a hundred billion years probably. To put that into perspective, the universe is less than fourteen billion years old."

"Ooh! What else?"

"Let me see... The light from stars takes millions of years to reach Earth, so when you look at them, you're literally looking back in time. Neutron stars are the densest and tiniest stars in the known universe. Although they have a radius of only about six miles, their mass might be denser than that of the sun, and they can spin as fast as seven hundred times per second. That's got to make you feel pretty dizzy after a while."

She seemed to delight in each fact. Her head was tilted right back, and he watched her face and glowed with pride. He racked his brain for a few more facts.

"If you think this pool of water is big," he said, "there's a water vapor cloud that holds one hundred forty trillion times the mass of water in the Earth's oceans. It's around ten billion light-years away. And if you think sulfur water smells funny, think again. Based on studies of dust at the center of our galaxy, the amino acids there suggest it most likely tastes like raspberries and smells like rum! And that's your humble space nerd's guide to the galaxy."

He hoped he hadn't been too nerdy. He'd been accused of that before. She whooped with joy, and he looked over at her with a big grin on his face.

"OK, you know your stuff," she said. "And I bet you can find what you're searching for if you look hard enough. I think the truth is right here. It's up there, and it's inside you."

Was she joking?

"Shall I eat another mushroom from my pocket to help me see it?" he said playfully.

"Definitely not. You've loosened up your mind with psychedelics, meditation, and yoga. Now it's time to focus. The mushrooms were just a tool. Like a telescope. The astronomer still needs to do the hard thinking. Look up at the sky. What do you see?"

She was serious.

"I see stars," he said. "And the moon."

"What else?"

"Space? A cloud?"

"And?"

He looked up, straining his eyes. "Nope, that's all."

"What about nearer, in the frame?"

"Ah, well, I see the trees here in this glade."

"Good. What else?"

"My eyebrows! I can kind of see my two furry eyebrows. Myself."

"Good, OK, you see stars, clouds, trees, and yourself. Now try to connect all of those things. How are they related?"

"I guess they're all made of atoms, the same basic building blocks. Let's start with the trees, which take in molecules, breaking them down to grow branches and leaves. The tree is fed by light that has traveled almost one hundred million miles through space from the sun. It builds new molecules from carbon dioxide and water, giving out oxygen and also some water as it does so. I stand here, breathing in the oxygen that the trees have created, eating their fruit and berries. Some of those water molecules ultimately end up in those clouds, which also protect me from the sun and provide water for the trees. I'm working all of this out in my brain, which is the most complex thing in the known universe but also mainly water. It's all connected. Just the same atoms flowing around forever."

"Exactly. And can you explain what's happening inside all of those atoms? What do we know?"

"OK, now you're pushing it! I don't think I can remember all of that."

"Try. It's important."

"Well, atoms are all made up of three particles: electrons, protons, and neutrons. But when you look closer, they're mostly space. In fact, I think they're almost a 100 percent space. It's difficult for the human mind to understand, but when you knock on a table, it's almost all empty space. If you zoom in even deeper, the protons and neutrons are made up of even smaller particles called quarks, which all have fancy names. And that's about what we know so far. When you get down to that level, it's called the quantum level. Things start to behave in weird and wonderful ways, depending on whether you look at them as waves or particles. I never quite understood the rules of the quantum universe."

She told him to keep going.

"I'm not sure I *can* go further," he said. "I love science, but I'm not a scientist, and I don't think we really need to know much more detail than that. When we try to study the subatomic level, we find things are ruled by probabilities rather than certainties, which means we just don't know. As humans, we like to deal with certainties and absolutes, not probabilities. We hate the idea that there's something we can never quite know. But many of the fundamental rules of nature are governed by the laws of chance, not certainty. The building blocks themselves turn out to be unknowable."

"You're saying that after thousands of years of scientific research, we still don't know the truth? So, what *can* we actually know by studying nature?"

He knew he was about to start talking again, but he had no idea what he was going to say. He knew that she was listening and that if she had questions, he would somehow have answers.

He would somehow find answers. "You mentioned Feynman earlier. Do you know what he said about nature and truth? He once said, 'Nature uses only the longest threads to weave her patterns, so that each small piece of her fabric reveals the organization of the entire tapestry.' I keep coming back to this picture of a giant cloth with endless threads. I sometimes feel like I'm one of those threads. Perhaps the most important truths are what we learn about *ourselves* when we study a small piece of the fabric of nature."

"Go on."

"Well, first of all, humility. We learn that we're just an insignificant collection of fluid atoms. We learn how impossibly against all the odds our very existence is. I mean, what are the odds that in all of these trillions of stars, across billions of years, this collection of atoms would combine at this moment to create you and me? As Carl Sagan said, extinction is the rule and survival is the exception. Think of all my thousands of ancestors that had to not get eaten or murdered for me to be here today. My improbability is deeply humbling.

"Second, connection. We learn we're connected to everybody and everything in the universe, all swimming in the same flow of atoms and forces. We are all made of the same stuff. We are more similar than we are different.

"And third, uncertainty. We now know that uncertainty rules the very heart of the universe, so we should never be surprised if daily life escapes our control. How can we expect certainty in life if it doesn't even exist within an atom?

"By studying the thinnest threads of nature, we learn all of these truths about the tapestry and about ourselves: humility, connection, uncertainty. Staying connected to nature keeps us rooted and closer to the truth."

The girl gasped. "That's seriously beautiful. Keep going. You're breaking through with something here. It's brilliant."

"That's all I have, but I'm glad you like it," the boy said with pride.

"No, you're not there yet. Make the connection. Your three truths. To you and me. Keep going."

Was there more? How did she know?

And then he saw something.

"I think I see it," he said. "It all connects with your three minds, right? They're all part of the same cloth. I mean, think about it. The three minds: grateful, compassionate, and observing. They're all reflections of the three truths we learn from nature: humility, connection, and uncertainty. It all fits together like a jigsaw puzzle. Humility leads us to gratitude. Connection leads us to compassion. Uncertainty leads us to observation. That's it. All the time we spend in nature, studying each piece of her fabric, can lead us to these truths that will permanently strengthen our minds."

CHOICE OF NATURE

LOOK DEEP INTO
NATURE TO FIND...

HUMILITY
CONNECTION
UNCERTAINTY

... AND STRENGTHEN
YOUR MIND...

GRATEFUL
COMPASSIONATE
OBSERVING

.CONNECT WITH NATURE TO KEEP
ROOTED AND CLOSER TO THE TRUTH

"Yes!" she cried. She was more excited than he'd ever seen her. "You've done it. I always knew the three minds were true somehow, but I never quite knew why. You've just rooted them forever in nature. I only need to study a fragment of the universe to feel connected to the three minds. I only need to look hard at a beautiful petal or a beetle to feel humility, connection, and uncertainty, which will strengthen my mind."

Her face glistened in the moonlight, steam rising and curling up her neck. He felt exhausted but proud. It had all fallen into place tonight. He pictured the tapestry and the threads, and the lines of a poem came to his lips:

The blue and the dim and the dark cloths
Of night and light and the half light

She almost jumped out of the water. "What did you say?"

"They're just some lines from a poem. Something about the cloths of heaven. I remember only those two lines, I'm afraid. We learned it at school. The tapestry reminded me of them. Why?"

She looked white in the moonlight. "It's…just…a very special poem to me. It's by Yeats. 'Aedh Wishes for the Cloths of Heaven.' Pa sang it to me every night in bed before I went to sleep."

He smiled, but she still looked shaken.

"Pa always told me it was written just for me," she continued, "and then I used to dream about the boy who wrote it. I was young, and I hoped one day he'd come find me. I kept coming back to that dream, especially whenever I was struggling."

She closed her eyes and recited the poem:

Had I the heavens' embroidered cloths,
Enwrought with golden and silver light,
The blue and the dim and the dark cloths
Of night and light and the half light,
I would spread the cloths under your feet:
But I, being poor, have only my dreams;
I have spread my dreams under your feet;
Tread softly because you tread on my dreams.

"It's beautiful."

She tilted her chin. "Do you want to kiss me?"

"I think I do."

"If you kiss me, will it make things better or worse?"

He had no idea.

He leaned in and kissed her once, knowing it might be both the first and last time.

They sat and watched the sky in silence, then dressed and walked back through the forest and across the meadow to the tent.

Choice of Attention

He normally felt anxious in the mornings, but today he felt lighter. He decided to read through his notebook before leaving the tent. He wanted to make sure he hadn't missed anything important.

He had pages of sketches and notes, and at the back of the notebook he kept a line for each idea:

> *The Path* – Take a path and walk it with a good mind and good choices.
>
> *The Grateful Mind* – Savor it all, every day, and always feel lucky.
>
> *The Compassionate Mind* – We must care and do more if possible, and it's always possible.
>
> *The Observing Mind* – Neither chase nor avoid things but accept them and be there in the middle.

Choice of Plan – Pick a few big rocks each day and tackle them first.

Choice of People – Find the many people who are good for you now and the few people who want the best for you forever.

Choice of Meditation – Sit still in the moment and observe each passing thought and sensation without judgment.

Choice of Body – Eat less, mainly plants; sweat; stretch; and sleep.

Choice of Nature – Connect with nature to keep rooted and closer to the truth.

It still made sense so far, but he wouldn't know if he could use it all until he heard the rest of it. He could see the final item on the girl's list was choice of wealth. That would be critical for him. Unless he had a way of at least supporting himself, everything else would be pointless.

He unzipped the tent and climbed out into the cool air. He joined the girl by the campfire, where she was boiling some water. They agreed to start the day with both yoga and meditation beneath the willow tree. He wanted to practice what he'd learned the day before. She gently guided him through the routines, which already felt less daunting to him.

At the end of the meditation session, she guided him through a new technique that she called sympathetic joy for others. First, they each imagined a good friend. They silently wished this friend joy and pictured them experiencing happiness. Then they switched their attention to a neutral person, wishing joy and happiness to someone they didn't know well. Then, after a few minutes, they switched again, now wishing joy to a difficult person, perhaps even an enemy. He immediately thought of Claudia and Jonah, back at the apartment. It was tough at first, but he managed to wish them joy and happiness together without sparking anger. He was surprised that he could do it. They ended the session by wishing joy to themselves and finally the whole world.

It took only a few minutes, but he could see its power immediately. He was starting the day feeling strong.

After a light breakfast, they set off down the path. They agreed to cover the last four choices today, starting with the choice of attention.

"I've been looking forward to this discussion," he told her. "I'm far too easily distracted. I need all the help I can get."

"I've seen you check your phone every hour or so since I met you."

He blushed. "Really?" He put his hand on his pocket.

"Yes, you did it right after our meditation this morning. Can you take it out for a moment?"

He took his phone out, feeling a bit nervous about it.

She took it from him. "May I keep it and use it for the rest of the day?"

He reluctantly agreed. His was heart racing.

"You look ill," she said, holding up the device. "What's wrong? How are you feeling?"

"It's dumb, I know, but I feel physically sick just at the

idea of not having it with me and letting someone else use it. Even though I trust you, my whole nervous system seems to be freaking out about it."

"And how does that make you feel?"

"Quite sad. Like an addict, I guess. Which I am. I call out other people for being obsessed with their screens, but I'm really no better."

The phone vibrated in her hand, and a message appeared on the screen with a chime. He could read it from where he stood. Claudia had texted him about paying the rent.

His chest tightened. He desperately wanted to ignore the message. But why was she still messaging him about the rent? They'd sorted it out. This was typical of her. He caught himself growing angry. *OK, forget this now. Focus. Back to the conversation.*

The girl looked at the screen before it dimmed. "Sorry!" she said. "Would you like your device back now? Do you need to deal with that? I was only using it to make a point."

He took it from her and turned it off. He stuffed it into his pack, where he hoped he wouldn't think about it. It felt dirty now, contaminating everything it touched.

"No, it's fine," he said. "I need to hear this. How do you avoid getting distracted? Do you even use technology?"

"I have an old device somewhere at the bottom of my pack. I haven't seen it for days, but I don't use it much. It's useful for emergencies, but I otherwise keep it out of sight and out of mind. I know if I don't control it, it will control me. I used to be addicted. I was terrified I would miss out on something more important than whatever I was doing. I'd consult it more often than I'd consult myself. I couldn't think straight for more than a few minutes without getting distracted. And then I got lucky."

"Lucky how?"

"At the start of the meditation retreat, we had to switch off and lock up all of our devices. For ten days, we had no screens, no radio, no books. It was tough at first, but soon it was a relief, and by the end of the ten days, it was very clear to most of us that we needed to make changes to take back control of our lives. When they handed it back at the end, the sight of it made me feel sick. I didn't turn it back on for a week. I knew it was my chance to take back control, before it hijacked my attention again. I could see it for what it was."

"And what exactly could you see?"

"That it's a very powerful and seductive tool that my brain isn't capable of resisting on its own without help. My brain was designed for a simpler environment. It was designed for when our ancestors lived closer to nature, where they needed to stay alert and anxious about direct and imminent threats. Early man always had to be ready to fight, fly, or freeze whenever there was a sign of danger. That probably happened at least a few times a day, but today we respond to way more stimuli through our devices. Our brains can't make these kinds of decisions ten thousand times a day. Our brains can't adapt fast enough. We're losing the battle for our own neurons."

"So what happened after the retreat?"

"I went back to the city and saw how people weren't protecting their attention carefully. I saw an 'infobesity' epidemic, information overload, junk information on every screen, just like the junk food and cheap carbohydrates tempting us on every supermarket shelf.

"I realized that our attention is the most valuable resource we have. We need to pay attention to where we pay attention. Our attention becomes our intention, and yet we give it away for free as if it had no value. We give it away to whoever shouts the loudest for it. I realized it's more precious than money because we can always get more money, but we can never get our attention back again."

"That's true. What did you do about it?"

"I just sat down and dedicated a day to making my new choices, and then I made big changes. I took a piece of paper and wrote down a simple plan under two columns: find the best and cut the rest.

"Under 'find the best,' I listed everything I wanted to give my attention to. I chose genres of books I knew would sharpen my mind and reveal important truths. Stoic philosophers. Classic biographies. Science classics. Shakespeare's plays. The simplest explanations of important truths, the original sources. And not just books. I also chose films, music, audio and essays by big thinkers.

"Under 'cut the rest,' I listed everything I wanted to avoid and delete. I drafted a long list of all the TV shows and technology habits that had been stealing my attention for years. I deleted almost everything and gave away most of my devices. I realized that the main aim of a TV show or channel is to get you to watch more TV. I stopped binge-watching trashy series about vampires, serial killers and drug cartels. I even cut out daily news and politics."

"That sounds extreme. Don't you miss knowing what's happening in the world?"

"Actually, that was the easiest thing to cut. It gave me a

lot of time back for more important things. The news is only one narrow view of what's happening in the world anyway. It always comes with an agenda, and it's not like I have a direct impact on the outcomes of the stories. I can only spectate—and often in pain. In my experience, people almost always treat each other well, but that isn't what the news shows. Bad news is good business. If it bleeds, it leads. We get the news we deserve."

"What about gaming? Computer games are dangerously addictive. I bet they didn't make the cut either."

"I'm not addicted to games, but I understand why people sometimes need to play them. In moderation, they serve a purpose. Think about it. Modern life is like a slow and highly frustrating game. We never quite know the aim or the rules. We don't know if we've reached the final level, or even if there is an endpoint. It's hard to distinguish our friends from our opponents. The game of life is so frustrating; it's no surprise we need to create games with clear rules and faster rewards. We need to invent games that have achievable goals and a sense of progress. It's how we cope with life."

He was feeling inspired to go through the same exercise. "I think I'm going to miss following the news, but I'll try it for a week. It's worth a test," he said. "Besides, we have to take control of our attention because things are going to get a whole lot more distracting soon."

"How so?"

"I worry about what's coming next. If we think screens and games are addictive now, we should be very worried about the future. Soon we'll all be able to choose between the reaworld and any number of virtual worlds. The real world isn't going to be a forgiving place to people without meaningful jobs, but virtual worlds will feel ever more rewarding to live in. I'm worried that people will emigrate into their machines. They'll be able to find excitement, joy, status, achievement, and even love inside their games. But it won't be real. It will be even further from the truth than ever."

"I hope you're wrong, but I fear you're right. Have you decided what you're going to write in your notebook yet?"

He had the line already in his head. "Choice of Attention – Find the best and cut the rest."

"It's brutally simple. It needs to be. I like it."

Choice of Making

"Shall we leave the path and explore the meadow for a while?" the girl asked. "It's a little slower, but the long grass is full of surprises, and it's good to try something new."

He followed her into the grass, and soon they were clambering over rocks. They sidestepped burrows and sent surprised birds high up into the air.

"Tell me what you used to do when you were seven years old and bored," she said.

"At seven? I don't remember. I liked my bike. I liked computer games."

"Right, but what about when there were no games, no TV shows, no other kids? Just you. What did you do?"

"Well, I know I used to draw my own comics because my mother kept them in a box somewhere for years. Apparently, I sat for hours making comics, mainly superhero stories."

He felt awkward talking about it, but she urged him on.

"The best comic was about a team of bears. They called Ten Bears, and they each had a superpower that they used to save whole cities. There was a grizzly bear, a polar bear, a panda bear. It was totally dumb, but somehow it worked. Other kids in my class used to read them and laugh their heads off. I was always shy, and I didn't show them to most people, but people loved them. Oh, yeah, and there was even a teddy bear and a gummy bear called Gummy. I can't remember what Gummy's superpower was though."

They both laughed.

She looked over at him and smiled. "Guess what?"

"What?"

"Just now, when you talked about something you created, your whole energy changed. Everything about you lit up. Have you ever thought about making comics again?"

"Ha! Never. I got too busy with school. I wouldn't know where to start now. I just forgot about it and it died."

She put her hand in his while they walked. "I think we all let something from our childhood die. We stop making the things we once loved to make. Artists often talk about trying to rediscover the moments they first saw something as a child. Picasso said, 'All children are artists. The problem is how to remain an artist once he grows up.'"

"That's sad. And probably true."

"People get to the end of their lives and don't even know why they stopped making things. They just wish they hadn't stopped because it was the thing that gave them the most joy. I think the day we stop is the day we become old. But we don't need to stop, and we can start again whenever we choose to. You could start again. You could look through the eyes of a seven-year-old again and add all of your new life experiences and start creating again. That's the next choice, the choice of making."

He already had several questions. "You mentioned Picasso. Are you only talking about art?"

"No, it can be anything we make for its own sake. It could be painting, music, writing, dance, a game, a sculpture, a vase, a dress, a cake. Anything. Anything we make because we want to, not because we have to. Some people have no idea what they're capable of. That's why we should give all children the chance to try everything at least once. Genius is evenly distributed around the world, but sadly the chance to pursue it isn't. History might have given us countless Picassos, but we have discovered only one so far."

"I'm feeling inspired to make something already."

She skipped a little with joy. "That's the whole point. Making things is exciting, and that excitement is contagious. We feed off each other and give each other permission to create. Unlike most things, creativity is limitless and can never run out."

"OK, but what about overcoming fear? Isn't that the hardest part, the fear of being judged by others, of failure?"

She squeezed his hand and pulled him down onto his knees to inspect the ground. "Check out this beetle here. Or this worm. These guys can't afford to fail. If they fail, they die. We're the only species that reaches for the stars and can afford to keep failing. You should fear only your own impotence, the things you *don't* make. Only you can allow others to judge you. As Georgia O'Keeffe put it, 'Flattery and criticism go down the same drain and I am quite free.'"

"But how do you even know what to make?"

"You can't find it if you don't look, so you have to start by starting. When I was young, I used to write songs, so I began writing again a few years ago. I'm still finding my voice, but I try to write at least something every day. There's new material everywhere when you look. Meditation helped me hear my words again. Nature showed me new truths to write about. I often dream about a song and then write down my dreams. The writing helps me lose myself and find myself at the same time. Here's how I look at it. Nobody really knows me, including myself, so if I just make my unknown known, I will always say something only I can say."

"Whenever I try to make something, I end up copying people I admire. I get paranoid about stealing ideas. That's probably just me."

She laughed. "Ha! I'm a total kleptomaniac. I'm an international idea thief. I believe no idea belongs to anybody, and I steal them with pride. Creativity is just connecting things. The artist scans the world for all the odd socks that belong together. It's not important where we take things from; it's where we take them to. We glorify originality, but we should actually celebrate theft. Bad artists copy; good artists steal." Her eyes blazed with mischief.

"OK, but why do we have to make something for its own sake? Why can't we make something to sell?"

"Intrinsic motivations make us happier than extrinsic ones. The kid who learns the piano because her parents force her to never quite plays with the same soul as the kid who chooses to play for herself. There's nothing wrong with selling a painting or a song, but the moment you start second-guessing what people will buy, it's work, not art. It's business. When you make things for others, you lose what made it authentic, and when it stops feeling true to you, it will stop feeling true to others. As long as it's for you, it's real art. And real artists don't starve."

They were back near the path now. They were tired after meandering through the tall grass and were now ready to rest and eat. They found two large boulders to sit on by the stream. They kicked off their boots and dipped their feet into the icy water.

They talked a little more while he scribbled in his notebook. He tried to capture everything into a single line. Finally, he declared victory.

"'Choice of Making – Make what only you can make, fearlessly and only for yourself.'"

She rewarded him with a hug and a slice of apple.

"Your book is almost finished," she said. "Does it have a name yet?"

"It's not my book; it's yours."

"It's ours."

After eating, they sat on the boulders and worked on their own projects. He started to sketch out the first frames of a new comic, while she worked on the next few lines of a song.

Choice of Helping

It felt good to rest their voices and their feet, but his toes started to feel numb in the cold stream. He swung his legs out and laid them on the bank.

"Let me warm them up," she said. She wrapped them in a towel and started massaging his feet.

"Thank you." He laughed. "I wasn't expecting that." He then offered to do the same for her.

"I'm actually borrowing your toes to help explain my choice of helping. You're the only person here, and it always makes me happy to help others. It's the rent we pay to live on Earth."

"I like that idea. How much rent should we pay and how often?"

"We should always try to help others without reason, hesitation, or expectation. That's my philosophy."

"Like when you ran back to return the wallet to that couple we passed the other day? That was definitely without reason, hesitation, or expectation. It sounds simple enough."

"That was just returning a wallet, but it's not always so simple. The world is usually grey, not black and white, which is why I like to remember my philosophy. It's easy to feel overwhelmed by suffering in the world and to do nothing about it. I often worry about the futility of trying to make a difference. I imagine what it's going to feel like to help one person and ignore another, and so I freeze up and do nothing. I get analysis paralysis."

"That's me!."

"Even worse, when I do help somebody, I wonder deep down whether I'm really doing it for them or doing it to look good and feel happy about myself."

"That's me! I want to change, but do you really believe it's even worth it given all the suffering in the world? Can we make a difference?"

"In Africa, they say that if you think you're too small to make a difference, try spending a night in a room with a few mosquitos. Everything makes a difference. Let me explain how."

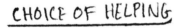

She picked up a thin branch and drew three concentric circles in the muddy bank of the stream. She labeled the inner circle "me," the next circle "you," and the outer circle "others." She then tossed the stick away and resumed massaging his feet while she spoke.

"Here's how it works. First is *me*. When I help others, it also helps me, whether I want it to or not. Nobody can stand living a meaningless life, and helping other people is the simplest way to give life more meaning. I sometimes receive payback, either directly or indirectly, when others notice and reward my kindness. It's never the reason *why* I help others, but it's often how the world works.

"Second is *you*. When I help you, for instance, with even the smallest gesture or the simplest of kind words, you will probably value it far more highly than I would expect. It's disproportionate. It's so easy to give and yet quite valuable to receive.

"Third is *others*. Never underestimate the ripple effect your kindness can have on a whole community if you inspire people around you to also help others. When people receive help, they learn to give help. They often pay it forward. A single act of kindness can scatter seeds on the wind, growing new flowers everywhere."

The more he stared at the three rings, the more it made sense. *Me. You. Others.* "OK, but I have questions. You say you help people without reason, but why? Surely it's better to focus your efforts on the most deserving cases?"

"I try not to look for a reason. Kindness itself is the only motive I need. It's great to see billionaire philanthropists tackling problems to save millions of lives, but I don't have the knowledge or power to play that game, and I know I'd overanalyze things. If I start to look for reasons or start weighing up the merits of different actions, I'll end up doing nothing. I don't need a reason, so I just help whoever's in front of me if I can. In fact, the less reason there is for helping somebody, the greater the surprise they feel. The greater the surprise, the more joy. The more joy, the more likely they are to feel inspired to go out and help others. In other words, the bigger the ripple."

"I've never thought of it like that before. It's almost a paradox: the less reason, the greater the impact. It's beautiful. But what about the second part, without hesitation? Why that?"

"Again, it's very simple. When we commit to helping others without hesitation, we overcome our tendency to overthink things. How often have you seen somebody who needed help, but the moment passed by the time you decided to help? Just help, without hesitation."

"It could go wrong though. You could help the wrong person altogether."

She laughed and squeezed his toes. "Now you're afraid of being recklessly helpful?"

"I'm overthinking it, right? OK, so what about the last part, without expectation?"

"That's also important. I used to help people only when I expected something in return. When I realized this, I stopped expecting anything in return. I was pleased with myself for a while, but I noticed I still had an expectation. I expected other people to at least be grateful, to say thank you to me. It was still all about me, and that was a problem. So now

I've worked out a solution. I've discovered the joy of helping people who will never find out that I helped them."

"Like a masked superhero."

"Sure, but my superpowers are pretty simple. I leave flowers on doorsteps. I tidy up yards at night. I leave a greeting card for the next person to use a coffee shop table. It's hard to believe, but it's even more fulfilling when nobody knows it's me."

It was the goofiest and most beautiful idea he'd ever heard. She was irrepressibly joyful, and he loved her for it. He captured it, exactly as she'd said the line, and read it out loud: "'Choice of Helping – Help others without reason, hesitation, or expectation.'"

He had one last question. "What if I can't find anybody to help? What if everybody's happy?"

"Don't worry about that. We're all fighting battles. We all need help from others."

Lost & Found

They put their boots back on and started off down the path again. Clouds clung to the mountain peaks above them, and a breeze swept through the valley.

After an hour or so, they saw a tall man walking along the path toward them. He was much older but handsome, with blond hair and crystal blue eyes. As he approached, they could see he was distraught.

"Have you seen my dog?" he asked in a thick European accent. "He's called Onyx. He's black, with a collar, and about so high." He held his hand out just below his waist.

They said they were sorry, that they hadn't seen poor Onyx. The boy told him they would definitely look out for him. The man started to write down his contact details for them in case they saw him, but his hands trembled, and his eyes filled with tears.

"I'm sorry," he cried. "I know he's just a dog, but I'm totally lost without him. He's all I have. He's the only one here for me, and I desperately need to find him."

The man's anguish was painful to watch.

The girl touched his arm softly. "I'm so sorry for you. I can't imagine your anxiety. I'll join you until you find Onyx."

The boy was shocked by her promise. What was she thinking? He signaled her to step away so they could talk privately.

When they were out of earshot, he said, "What are you doing? You can't just wander off with a complete stranger to look for a dog. We don't even know if Onyx actually exists. This guy could be an axe murderer."

"Well I've been wandering with you, haven't I? You haven't murdered me with an axe yet."

"Come on, be serious for once. We don't know this guy," he said.

"I'm sorry, but we do know he's in pain. He needs to find his dog while it's still light. There are mountain lions and coyotes out on the mountain. I can see he's suffering. I need to help him."

"But what about me? What about us? We haven't even finished all the choices."

"Of course, I would prefer to carry on walking with you, but his need is greater than yours right now. You understand the path, the minds, and most of the choices now. We will find each other again. I'm sorry, but I need to help him find his dog." She held out her arms.

"I thought we were on a special journey together," he said.

He stood rigid while she hugged him goodbye. She then took the blond man by the elbow, and they began walking back the way they'd come. She turned to wave, but the boy couldn't wave back. Then, in a panic, he called out after her.

"Hold on! Why don't I come with you? I can look for the dog. Wait for me."

But she didn't hear and didn't turn around again, and he

stood there stiff and rooted. He was too proud to run after her. Moments later, she and the man disappeared behind a bend in the path.

Where was her so-called compassion? How could she abandon him like this?

First, he'd lost his father, then Claudia, and now her.

Why hadn't he just walked straight to climb the rock face? How—?

And then he caught himself. His anger was feeding off itself again. He took a deep breath. He saw how his thoughts were thinking themselves. He had become attached to the girl, and he feared losing her. Just a few days ago, he didn't know she even existed, but now he couldn't imagine life without her.

He was alone in the meadow now. He tried to imagine what she would do in his shoes, line by line.

His grateful mind thanked her for all the valuable lessons she had shared with him.

His compassionate mind hoped they'd find Onyx fast and that this would ease the man's suffering.

His observing mind accepted the power of his feelings, sat with them, and refused to be judgmental for having them.

He remembered her choice of helping and shook his head. Just an hour ago, he was completely ready to help others without reason, hesitation, or expectation, and yet all of his selfish instincts took over when a stranger needed help.

He still had a long way to go, and he could see it.

He'd fallen deeply in love with the girl, but he wasn't ready to be with someone like her. He didn't deserve her. She'd given him a framework and all the tools to flourish, but he still hadn't learned how to use them. She was right, though, he didn't need her anymore; he needed to grow up through careful practice and dedication. He decided to sit awhile and meditate before walking on again.

Eyes closed, he focused on his natural breath, gently flowing in and out gently from his nostrils.

He felt his breath touch his skin, the hairs on his upper lip, sometimes cool, sometimes warm.

Inhaling, he focused on his breath. Exhaling, he listened to the gentle noises of the meadow.

He worked hard to note his thoughts as they arose and faded, not judging them or clinging to them. He just observed.

He was deep into his meditation when he sensed someone was nearby. He opened his eyes to find the girl seated in front of him, also meditating. The curl of a smile was on her lips.

"You're back!" he whispered with delight.

She opened her eyes and started to laugh. She crawled to him and hugged him tightly.

"Look at you!" she said. "I left for only a while, and here you are already seated like a little Buddha. I almost decided to leave you to your stillness. My work here with you is clearly done."

He begged her not to leave again and asked what had happened with the search. She explained how they'd found Onyx just a mile down the path. The man and his dog were overjoyed by their reunion.

"Well, I'm glad you came back," the boy said. "You've taught me a lot in just a few days. I could walk and listen to you talk forever. I panicked at first when you left. I can't imagine why you'd want to spend so much time with me. I've never met anyone who can talk like you."

"And I've never met anyone who can listen like you." Her head was on his shoulder. "I don't always know what I'm going to say until I hear myself say it. I think by talking. I can't talk if nobody listens, which means I can't really think unless someone listens. You don't know this yet, but you have a special gift for listening. You hear me, and you make me better. You say I've taught you a lot, but your questions and your open mind have taught us both."

He felt she was just being polite and told her so.

"No, you need to understand this. Nothing is more important. I can't talk and think properly if you don't listen," she repeated.

"People will always listen to someone like you. They just do."

"Most people pretend to listen. Very few actually do. Most people already have their beliefs, or their religion already fixed in their heads. Just think about the people you know in your own life. How many of them actually sit down and really listen?"

She was right. Very few did.

"I hope you're not telling me you're lonely," he said. "You have the best life in the world. You have the freedom to go wherever you want. I want your life. Tell me you're not miserable like all the rest of us, please!"

"You're right. I'm healthy and free. When you don't allow yourself to be tied down by thick roots, you can walk through life with a special kind of lightness. I've been able to work out a lot of important things. But sometimes I wish I had someone who stayed around, someone to talk with, to read with. I'm free to go anywhere, but I also don't belong anywhere."

Choice of Wealth

To pass the time as they walked, the boy asked the girl to share her songs. She self-consciously sang a few verses. The lyrics were distinctively hers.

They saw smoke rising up ahead at a bend in the stream. They came across an old woman in a tattered straw hat. She was seated in a low chair in front of a small fire. She smiled and waved at them to join her. There was some food laid out on a small table next to her.

"I have berries, nuts, and mushrooms I foraged from the forest," she said happily, "and I've made some fresh tea. There's plenty for everyone! Take what you need! Pay what you can!"

They were hungry, so they sat on the ground next to her and tried a bit of everything. She told them she'd lived in the valley for decades, and she shared stories about the changing seasons.

"I love meeting young couples like you two, but I like winter best, when I'm all alone with the snow, the trees, and the animals." She chuckled.

After they'd eaten and were ready to leave, they thanked their host and stuffed some money into a rusty can on the table.

"This is the freshest food I've ever eaten," the boy said, as he left. "You should open up a store in San Francisco." He was only half-joking.

The woman looked confused. "Why?"

"Where I live, we all go to farmers' markets for fresh food, but yours is better. You have a forest market here. You could call your store The Forest Market. Wild plants and teas. Big green letters. I've even got a tagline: 'It doesn't get fresher than this.' Or 'Where the wild things live.' I honestly think it would take off. You could charge a premium. High margins. You could franchise it out in every major city."

The woman looked even more confused and even a little sad. "And why would I want to do all of that?"

"Well…I guess to build a bigger business, make more profit," he explained quietly.

He now wished he'd kept the thought to himself. He was about to tell the woman she could sell her business one day and live anywhere she wanted, but he could see she was already exactly where she wanted to be.

The old woman sighed and waved them on.

A few minutes down the path, the boy said, "That was a bit awkward."

The girl laughed. "I think we're ready to learn the choice of wealth."

"I think you're right. Save me before I upset somebody else!"

"OK, let's start with the word *wealth*. What does it mean to you?"

"Wealth is all about making money, getting the skills to find a job, build a career, maybe start my own company. It's about working hard while I'm young, doing whatever it takes to make enough money to get a deposit for a house and a mortgage. Get a car, support a family, go on vacations, and such. It's about investing and about retiring one day. It's a lifetime of different things…"

He felt queasy as he heard himself describe it all. It daunted him. These were all things he hadn't even gotten started on yet.

"OK, you mentioned making money," she said. "Let's start with the difference between wealth and money. Wealth and money are two different things. Wealth is what you should pursue, not money. Wealth is about having options and not just having money. Wealthy people don't necessarily have the most money, but they always have *enough* money. You can't choose to be rich because money comes and goes, but you can usually choose to be wealthy because you get to decide how much is enough for you. Wealthy people also often have both time and money because they've worked out how to earn it by doing what they find easy. Even better, they earn money while they sleep."

"And they probably sleep very well!" he said. "That all makes sense, but I've seen lists of the world's wealthiest people, and they all have billions of dollars."

"Those are rich lists, not wealth lists. Who knows if those billionaires have enough money to make them happy? In fact, billionaires often say that when you get enough money to feel secure and free, you feel happier, but after that, more money only creates more responsibility and more worries. Money doesn't protect them from most of the problems that cause people to suffer, just a few of the obvious ones, such as the need for food, shelter, and medicine."

"You can have too much money, then?"

"Money is like fuel on a road trip. You never want to run dry, but the point of the road trip is not to visit gas stations."

He laughed out loud, but he needed more convincing.

"Try thinking of it as an addiction," she continued. "If you regularly eat a lot of sugar, your body craves more sugar. If you regularly smoke cigarettes, your body craves nicotine. Money is no different. If you focus your mind on money or you make yourself dependent on needing a lot of it, you will become addicted to acquiring more of it. People who work in finance often earn a lot of money, but they get too close to it and get addicted to it. As with any addiction, it can take over everything and make it hard to see the value in other things."

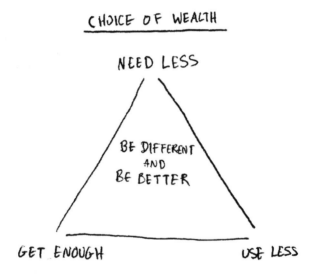

CHOICE OF WEALTH

NEED LESS

BE DIFFERENT
AND
BE BETTER

GET ENOUGH   USE LESS

SEEK WEALTH, NOT MONEY.
WEALTH IS ABOUT HAVING OPTIONS,
NOT JUST MONEY.

She stooped to pick up a handful of sticks and placed them carefully on a smooth patch of earth near the path. She used three sticks to form a triangle. Next to each corner, she wrote two words: *need less*, *use less* and *get enough*. "Wealth is what happens when three things align for you: When you *need* less, when you *use* less, and when you *get* enough. Think about it. There's no point spending your life obsessed about the pursuit of money if you're overwhelmed by an even stronger *need* for it and you *use* it wastefully. But if you find a way to *get* enough money easily, and you don't *need* much money, and then you invest and use it wisely, you can feel like the wealthiest person in the world."

He stared hard at the triangle, scratching his head like a cartoon character. The logic seemed far too simple to be true. Why didn't they teach this at school? "It all sounds interesting, but you still need to get some money from somewhere. Not everyone can endlessly wander in meadows like you. I don't mean to be rude, but normal people still need to find jobs and work."

She looked confused. "You think I don't know how to make money?"

"I'm sorry. I didn't mean it like that. I just assumed... because we haven't talked about it, and you never mentioned a job... I just assumed you'd inherited some money or something like that. That sounds terrible, I know. I can't really imagine you sitting at a desk working in an office."

She laughed. "I actually earn money from selling my songs. I don't usually talk about it unless I have to, but I probably should have told you before."

"What?"

"It's not a fortune, but it more than covers my needs. I write songs and send them to my friend who's an agent in LA. She takes care of all the licensing deals and contracts. She licenses them to musicians and for TV shows, ads, and movies. Apparently, one of my songs is being used in thirty countries around the world this summer."

He was in shock. She was wealthy?

"I live like a poor person with way too much money," she said. "I keep moving, so I don't pay rent or own a car. I don't wear makeup or jewelry. I hardly have any bills to pay. Wherever I go, I try to give back and serve at food banks. As long as I keep writing new songs that people enjoy and keep building my reputation, I don't think I'll ever need to work for money again."

He shook his head in disbelief. He was still saddled with debt. The fear and uncertainty of it always gnawed away like a rat at the back of his mind. He could feel his anger rising. He envied her because she had found her freedom already. Intellectually, he understood her point about focusing on wealth instead of money, but right now his whole being was wired to crave money. He needed it. A lot of it. As soon as possible. He would take it however it came.

He couldn't conceal the red patches on his cheeks as his anger rose, consuming him.

"I think my story has upset you," she said sadly. "Don't fight your feelings. Let them rise and gently fall. Thinking about money drives people mad, which is why I try to avoid the whole subject if I possibly can."

She saw right through him every time, he thought. Now his cheeks were red with shame.

"Ignore me," he said. "I'm just in awe—and a little jealous. I'll get over it. I just need to figure out how to do what you've done. I haven't even gotten started. How did you do it?"

She thought carefully. "I focused on being different and better at something, and I just stuck with it. Many people work hard, but very few are truly original. The world used to reward people who blended in. Now it rewards people who stand out. That's what my agent taught me. She told me to just be myself and make sure I write songs that are different and better. That's all I try to do. I deliberately live a unique kind of life and then turn it into music. My adventures become songs." She smiled. "My days with you will become a song or two, I'm sure. Perhaps a whole album!"

"I'd listen to that one!" He felt himself glowing with pride. "Different and better? I like that idea. I've spent my life trying to follow the rules and tick the boxes. But you're right. The world isn't looking for rule-followers. I need to stand up and stand out."

"Exactly. Making money used to be all about who you know. Now it's about what you can make. It takes skill or artisanship though. When I started writing my songs, they were awful. They sounded bland, just like every other song, and nobody wanted them. But I listened to my agent's advice and kept making them different and better. Eventually it clicked. I stuck with it and found my voice. People get too distracted and jump around trying too many things. When you're trying to polish one pebble to stand out on a beach of millions, it takes commitment and it takes skill."

He no longer felt jealous; he felt inspired. He already had a few ideas he wanted to try, and her story had filled him with the energy to pursue one of them. He was about to tell her, but she wasn't finished yet.

"Plus, there's a whole other path to take to find wealth," she said. "It may not sound as exciting as writing songs or building a new company, but it works for millions of people. <u>Many people find wealth by simply doing</u> a job they enjoy inside great companies. The same rule applies: Be different and better to stand out and succeed. After all, not everybody enjoys the risk and the relentless burden of starting something new."

Now he was confused again. Part of him wanted to know if he could succeed inside a big organization. Would he rise to the top or get stuck in the middle? He certainly needed more career experience, and he was already in debt. It wasn't the most adventurous choice, but it might be the most sensible way to get started.

Which path should he take? Was he more likely to find wealth trusting his own talent or working inside a company? Thinking about that choice always filled him with anxiety. He felt he was back at the crossroads, scratching his head.

It felt like an impossible question, but it also felt strangely familiar. Who else had spoken to him about that just recently? Then he remembered. It was the driver of the red Chevy who had brought him up the mountain.

"I had this same conversation on the drive up with an old guy in a pickup truck. He was maybe sixty, very sharp, but he'd just been laid off by his company again and was pissed about it. The truck reeked of bourbon. He may have been drinking. But he talked about the same question. He was debating whether he should try to find another job or strike out on his own."

"And what did he say about it?"

"He wasn't a big fan of companies, that's for sure. He said it's dangerous to bet your happiness on finding a safe job because they don't exist anymore. He'd worked in sales for a dozen companies in his life, and always did well, but looking back on his career, he'd never felt safe. He said no job is ever what it seems from the outside. Companies are constantly sold or merged. Teams get reorganized or laid off. New managers shake things up. New technology creates winners and losers. He'd spent his whole career either finding new positions or clinging onto his existing one, constantly looking over his shoulder."

"It sounds very stressful."

"Very, and he also talked about companies being psychopathic. I thought he was nuts at first, but it kinda started to make sense. He explained that corporations are treated as people in our legal system and yet they feel no empathy, guilt, or remorse. If they were in fact people, they would be diagnosed as psychopathic. They don't care about people. People in companies usually care about other people, but the company itself doesn't. The leaders of companies create beautiful mission stories to hide this fact, but if you study their actions, you'll find they care only about creating shareholder value. That's their reason for existence. If a company doesn't need you, it will cut you off, and you'll never hear from it again. Like a psychopath."

"Whoa, that's bleak. It sounds like he was ready to quit corporate life and strike out on his own then."

"Yes and no. That's the funny thing. He still had a lot of great memories working for companies. He'd met inspirational people, and some had become his closest friends. He had no regrets other than trusting in companies too much earlier in his career. For him, the *team* was the most important thing—not himself, not the company, but the team. I liked the way he talked about it."

"It sounds like he really cared about the people he worked with."

"He said if you work only for yourself, nobody will trust you. If you work only for your company, you're trusting a psychopath. But if you focus your efforts on the success and happiness of your team, you can't fail. At worst, you'll make new friends and great memories. People will love you for being a selfless manager and leader, and talented people will want to work for you. Either way, you can't fail."

They walked on in silence, both deep in thought.

There was a dance in the boy's step now. "I see two clear paths, and they both excite me. I can strike out on my own or find a team to join at a company where I can grow and be helpful to others. Very different, but two great choices, right?"

"Right! At least two. It sounds like you know what to write in your notebook now."

"I need to think first."

They walked on for a while longer. He then stopped and shared his line: "'Choice of Wealth – Need less, use less, be different, and be better.'"

She approved. She stopped abruptly on the path and put her arm in his, pulling him close.

"I forgot to tell you my secret rule for needing less." She laughed mischievously.

"Sure. But why are you laughing? Why do I get the feeling I'll regret hearing it?"

She cupped her hands to his ear as if it were a great secret. "Don't buy anything," she whispered.

"Don't buy anything? Don't you mean don't buy too much? I mean, unless you're begging or stealing your food, surely you have to buy *some* things..."

She laughed again. "Just don't buy anything."

"But I saw you buy food and tea from the old woman, at the forest market. That was something."

"That was an exception. I wanted to help her. And I was hungry," she said coyly.

"OK, but what about your backpack? Your boots? Your toothbrush?"

"I made an exception to buy my backpack. And the boots. And the toothbrush."

He waited for her to explain her logic, but she just grinned at him.

"So...am I missing something here? I don't get it. It sounds like you have to make a lot of exceptions. It sounds like 'Don't buy anything, apart from all the exceptions'"

"That's boring. I prefer *don't buy anything*. We always forget how little we need. Those three words remind me of that. Shall we keep walking now?"

He watched her walk off, almost floating down the path. He watched in awe. He'd never met anyone who moved and thought with such lightness before.

Getting Out of the Way

"I'm ready to stop here for the day if you are," the girl said.

He was. They had walked the last stretch in silence, and his mind had been racing. He couldn't stop thinking about the guide—one path, three minds, nine choices—trying to make sense of it all. He was eager to start using it all, but he still had questions.

"I'm almost out of food," she said. "Would you mind making camp while I forage in the trees before dark?"

When she left, he got to work. He pitched the tent and lit a fire. He sat and waited, boiling water and wondering how long she'd be gone. It was quiet without her, and his mind was galloping again. A creeping sense of anxiety started to rise in his chest. Where was she? What if she never came back?

He checked to see if her backpack was still there. It was over by the stream, which meant she was coming back. She wouldn't just leave him like that without saying goodbye, would she? Perhaps that's exactly how she'd leave him, now that they'd finished all the sections of the guide. When they first met, she said they'd cover only a few parts of it. She had already stayed with him longer than she had intended.

What would happen after she left? Would the guide still make any sense to him? He'd taken notes, but what if it didn't work for him like it worked for her? He could end up back where he'd started, alone on the bridge at night.

His head was spinning, his heart racing. A memory of his father in the hospital seized him. The matchstick limbs, the hollow gaze. A wave of sadness flooded in and tears welled up. He felt lost again. Why couldn't he move on from thinking about him? What if he never moved on, never got over it?

What if…?

The girl was gone forever…?

He screwed up the guide…?

The grief never died…?

What if…?

"Mushrooms, nuts, and berries! Plenty for everyone! Take what you need! Pay what you can!" cried the girl triumphantly, grasping her bulging shawl. "If only I had an old straw hat, I'd make a great foraging lady, I think." She laughed as she joined him cross-legged by the fire.

He looked up and tried to smile. She saw his panic. She saw everything.

"Hey, what's up?" she said. "You look like you saw a bear. Or ten bears."

He choked on a laugh. "I'm sorry. I'm fine. I just got hijacked by my thoughts again."

She smiled.

"I forgot everything you taught me," he said. "I let my

thoughts catch fire and rage. Next time, I'll be ready to observe and watch them rise and pass."

"How do you feel about everything we've discussed and what you've written down in your notes?"

"It's extraordinary. It all fits together, and I believe in it. Everyone should know about it."

"But...?"

He hesitated. He started to talk, but he didn't know what he was going to say. "But...I'm pretty sure I'm going to screw it all up. I'm going to wake up tomorrow and try to meditate and try to feel grateful and try to make all the good choices, and it's going to feel great for a while, maybe a week, but then it's going to stop feeling great. Then I'll be back here, panicking and thinking about my father and thinking about jumping off another cliff."

They sat in silence, staring into the flames. He was surprised at how much he'd shared, but she didn't seem to be.

"I have an idea," she said. "Grab your towel and follow me. I know a place that might help you to understand something, if you can work out how to get there."

She leapt up and helped him to his feet. They ran across the meadow and scrambled into the forest. They made their way up a steep path for a few hundred yards. The red dusk glowed through the canopy above, and they began to hear the sound of rushing water up ahead. The noise grew louder as they ran. At the end of the path, they stood looking down on a thundering waterfall. It formed a misty curtain for the deep cave behind it.

"It's awesome!" he shouted over the sound of the water. "Is it safe to jump in?"

She nodded that it was safe and challenged him to meet her in the cave behind the falls. He turned and clambered down, diving headfirst into the deep pool in his attempt to reach the cave first. She watched from above. He swam as hard as he could against the rushing water, but the closer he got, the harder it swept him back. He pushed harder, determined to swim through and beat her to the cave, but the force of the water was too strong, and he had to retreat. Three times he tried to fight his way through, and three times he was pushed back. He eventually conceded defeat, exhausted and a little disappointed.

"You swam as hard as you could!" she shouted.

"I wish I'd gone harder the first time!" he yelled. "I got weaker after every attempt."

She waded into the water and swam past him. She then turned onto her back and floated gently toward the waterfall. The force of the water pushed her backward, but instead of fighting against it, she floated face up on the surface. The power of the water swirled her body toward the side of the pool and then gently all the way behind the falling water and into the cave. Through the torrent, he could see her smiling face on the surface of the water. She glided like a feather.

He followed her, floating out on his back and allowing the swirling water to guide him around the falls. Soon, he too was in the cave. He marveled at the pink dusk shining through the wall of water.

"That actually felt good," he said, "just to let go and float for once."

"It's how we all started life. In the comfort of a womb, floating happily in the darkness. Once we enter the world, we spend the rest of our lives trying to learn how to float again."

"That was another lesson, wasn't it? You're about to tell me I've been trying too hard to fight against the current. You think I should just let go, don't you?"

She smiled. "It sounds like that's what *you* think."

"It felt so much easier your way, to just float where the water pushed us. But it goes against everything I've been told about how to succeed in life. All the famous and successful people say the same thing. If you want to be number one, you need to go out and fight for it. They never say they just floated around and let it happen."

"Do you want to be number one?"

"I honestly don't know anymore."

"Let's put it this way. Would you prefer an almost certain chance of being happy or a one percent chance of being number one?"

"That's easy. I'd choose to be happy."

"Then perhaps you're ready. Just get out of the way and let yourself flourish now. You know everything you need to know. Just be—and enjoy being. We're told that holding on makes us strong, but in truth it's letting go that gives us power. Just get out of the way."

"You keep saying that. Get out of the way of what?"

"You. Yourself."

Something twitched inside, like a key turning. *Me?*

"There are just too many people out there for you to please, or mountains to climb," she said. "You'll never climb them all, and even if you climb one, you'll find it's just a foothill compared to a much higher peak behind it. You have to choose to be enough and get out of the way. You have to choose to stop looking for a better *why*, or a better *where*, and start enjoying *how* you walk your path."

He felt a click, and a door inside him swung wide open. It felt like the missing piece. He had to repeat it, just to make sure.

"I have to get out of the way," he said, "and stop looking for a better *why*, or a better *where*, and start enjoying *how* I walk my path."

Yes.

"I just take a path and walk it with a good mind and good choices. And get out of the way."

Yes.

"If that's really all it takes, I think even I can manage that!"

The girl reached across and pushed a strand of hair out of his eyes. Could she still see the sadness in them?

"There's something else, isn't there?" she asked. "Why can't you get out of the way?"

He could smell the hospital. He felt his father's hollow gaze. "I can't stop thinking about my father, and it keeps setting me back. I'm terrified I'll never move on."

"How does that feel?"

"It feels like a giant hole that I keep falling into even though I know it's there every time. It's like I want to fall into the hole even though I also want to move on with my life. Does that sound right?"

"I know it's right," she said. "Last year, I lost a friend, and a giant hole opened up inside me. I blamed myself, and for months I kept falling into it. I finally just got tired of climbing out, and I learned to walk around it. The hole is still there, and it always will be. But now when I see it, the depth of the hole just reminds me of the depth of my love, and it fills me with joy. Grief is just another type of love."

"But it makes no sense at all that I'm still struggling. I wasn't even close to him. I think I was always a disappointment to him, and I'm not even sure he loved me."

"I'm sure he did."

"He never told me he did. Why can't I move on if he couldn't show his affection when he was around?"

"Not everyone has the ability to turn their love into affection. Perhaps you already know this and now it's time to accept it. You know he couldn't speak his love. Maybe that's why the hole is so deep. It's still a mile wide and a mile deep because he never knew how to fill it in while he was alive. Nobody taught him how to, so he just kept digging it, alone."

He knew all of it was true.

"I want a big hole inside me, so I never forget him," he said. "It will always be there, but at least I know where it is. I don't need to keep falling into it. I can walk around it and be grateful for everything he did for me. And I can be a better companion to my mother even though she says she doesn't need me."

She took his icy hand and interlocked her fingers into his.

"Do you want to kiss me?" he asked, surprising himself.

"I think I do."

"Wait!" He tried to remember her line from the night before. "If you kiss me, will it make things better or worse?"

She laughed. "I don't know." She floated against him and they kissed.

They were cold. It was time to head back, but there was something he had to tell her first.

"I know you need to be free and keep moving," he said.

"I'm grateful for what you've taught me, but I also know I'm not ready for you."

"Maybe it's me who's not ready yet. Nobody has ever listened to me like you do. It's changed me. I'm not sure I want to keep moving forever."

"Walking the path with you has changed my life forever."

"If we're on the path, we'll be together, wherever we are," she said.

Holding hands, they rolled onto their backs and floated out from behind the waterfall. They dressed and ran back through the moonlit forest and across the meadow to the warmth of the fire.

The Beginning

"Let me cook breakfast while you tune yourself up for the day ahead," the girl said, pointing to a nearby tree.

It was early, and the dew still clung to the long grass. The mist was still rising all down the valley.

The boy found a mossy seat by the tree and he closed his eyes. His practice was strong, and he was able to observe and accept each thought as it arrived and faded. The usual anxieties came, but he didn't cling to them. He sat with memories of his father for as long as he wanted to and then moved on. He was out of the way now, watching his own mind with playful curiosity. He sat perfectly still and drew energy from the ground beneath him and from the tree against his spine.

Finally, he allowed his mind to go where it wanted, to everything he'd learned over the past few days. He recalled the guide as he'd captured it line by line:

> *The Path* – Take a path and walk it with a
> good mind and good choices.

> *The Grateful Mind* – Savor it all, every day,
> and always feel lucky.

The Compassionate Mind – We must care and do more if possible, and it's always possible.

The Observing Mind – Neither chase nor avoid things but accept them and be there in the middle.

Choice of Plan – Pick a few big rocks each day and tackle them first.

Choice of People – Find the many people who are good for you now and the few people who want the best for you forever.

Choice of Meditation – Sit still in the moment and observe each passing thought and sensation without judgment.

Choice of Body – Eat less, mainly plants; sweat; stretch; and sleep.

Choice of Nature – Connect with nature to keep rooted and closer to the truth.

Choice of Attention – Find the best and cut the rest.

Choice of Making – Make what only you can make, fearlessly and only for yourself.

Choice of Helping – Help others without reason, hesitation, or expectation.

Choice of Wealth – Need less, use less, be different, and be better.

Getting Out of the Way – Stop looking for a better *why*, or a better *where*, and start enjoying *how* you walk your path.

Now he was ready for the world. He opened his eyes with a smile.

The fire crackled, but the girl wasn't there. He looked for her at the stream and then checked for her inside the tent. Back at the fire, he noticed her backpack was missing. He sat for a while and finally called out to the trees on all sides of the camp.

She was gone, possibly forever this time, but he wasn't afraid.

He then noticed that his notebook was open. A large black pebble rested on the page. She had left her details and below that just a few words:

Everything is possible again.
I will see you on the path.
Tread softly.

Your forever friend.

He looked into the fire.
Out of the corner of his eye, he saw a hummingbird flutter

busily between two red flowers. Now he understood their beautiful dance: The flower gave sweet nectar; the bird carried her pollen away in return. Each needed the other to flourish.

Closing his eyes, he imagined a row of chairs reserved for his forever friends. The girl was seated on one of them now. She sat there by his side as they watched the sunset.

He would walk and find others who needed him, until none of his chairs were empty.

- **THE PATH** - TAKE A PATH AND WALK IT WITH A GOOD MIND AND GOOD CHOICES.

THE GRATEFUL MIND - SAVOR IT ALL, EVERY DAY, AND ALWAYS FEEL LUCKY.

THE COMPASSIONATE MIND - WE MUST CARE AND DO MORE IF POSSIBLE, AND ITS ALWAYS POSSIBLE.

THE OBSERVING MIND - NEITHER CHASE NOR AVOID THINGS BUT ACCEPT THEM AND BE THERE IN THE MIDDLE.

CHOICE OF PEOPLE - FIND THE MANY PEOPLE WHO ARE GOOD FOR YOU NOW AND THE FEW PEOPLE THAT WANT THE BEST FOR YOU FOREVER.

CHOICE OF MEDITATION - SIT STILL IN THE MOMENT AND OBSERVE EACH PASSING THOUGHT AND SENSATION WITHOUT JUDGMENT

CHOICE OF BODY - EAT LESS, MAINLY PLANTS; SWEAT; STRETCH; AND SLEEP.

CHOICE OF NATURE - CONNECT WITH NATURE TO KEEP ROOTED AND CLOSER TO THE TRUTH

CHOICE OF ATTENTION - FIND THE BEST AND CUT THE REST.

CHOICE OF HELPING - HELP OTHERS WITHOUT REASON, HESITATION OR EXPECTATION

CHOICE OF MAKING - MAKE WHAT ONLY YOU CAN MAKE, FEARLESSLY AND ONLY FOR YOURSELF.

CHOICE OF WEALTH - NEED LESS, USE LESS, BE DIFFERENT, AND BE BETTER.

GETTING OUT OF THE WAY - STOP LOOKING FOR A BETTER WHY, OR A BETTER WHERE, AND START ENJOYING HOW YOU WALK YOUR PATH.

If you enjoyed reading *Path*,
please take a moment to leave a review.
Tell others how it helped you.

If you know people who would find *Path* helpful,
please lend or order them a copy today.

www.jechadwick.com

More about PATH:
A Practical Aid To Happiness

*The guide is real. It took me thirty years
to learn it the hard way. The next time you hit a wall or fall
into a hole, try it for a week or two. If it works,
stick with it. I call it PATH: a practical aid to happiness.
It's a simple guide to understand, but you will still need
to put in the effort to walk it, if you choose to.*
—from the Preface

Take a path and walk it with a good mind and good choices.

Find more resources or join the PATH community at jechadwick.com

**If you found the book and the guide helpful,
please help others discover their path by**
• leaving a review on Amazon or other websites, or
• gifting a copy to a friend who might benefit from it.

How to take action and use PATH in your daily life:
Practice the exercises in this book
Subscribe to the free newsletter
Join the Facebook community group
Download the free synopsis: "Path: The Journal Pages"
Follow on social media
Discover background sources

Acknowledgments

After collecting notes for more than twenty years, I found writing *Path* far easier than I had expected. Rewriting it, and rewriting it again and again, was harder than I could ever have imagined.

First, I thank my family for cheering me on to the final page: Jacinta, Thomas, John, Eddie, Lucy, and William. And especially my parents, Jean and David, for their unlimited capacity for love, laughter, and adventure.

Next, I thank my beta readers for their brutal honesty: Mel, Gerson, Hugo, Kyle, Bea, Scott, Jenny, Dave, Rob, Jules, Megan, Christa, Lewis, and Giles.

I also thank a few of my many teachers for their wisdom: Joel Altman, S. N. Goenka, Sam Harris, Yuval Noah Harari, Johann Hari, the 14th Dalai Lama, Wayne Dyer, Dr James Doty, Richard Feynman, Robert Wright, W. B. Yeats, and William B. Irvine.

Next, I thank my magical son Lawrence Perry for turning my simple words into beautiful pictures.

I am also grateful to some very clever publishing folks who helped turn a manuscript into a book: Coverkitchen, Dan, Holly, Anne, and Mary.

But most of all, I thank my readers for giving *Path* their valuable attention. I hope they find it helpful.

About the Author

J. E. Chadwick is a British author living in California. He wrote *Path* to help his four children and ten nieces and nephews find more happiness.

Always restless, he quit school to hitchhike across Europe and the Middle East, where he rented snorkels in Israel and ran a guesthouse in a Turkish cave. At Oxford University, he studied mythology and utopian literature. Then, for twenty-five years, he worked in more than a dozen countries. He started as a journalist in Hong Kong and joined Facebook as an early employee.

On his travels, he took thousands of pages of notes, hoping one day they would mean something. Then, after a ten-day silent meditation retreat in Java, the patterns in the notes became very clear, and he sat down to write *Path*.

More at www.jechadwick.com

To illustrate the book, Chadwick collaborated with his son, the artist Lawrence Perry. During the first few weeks of the Covid-19 pandemic lockdown, they made the most of their unexpected spare time to recreate the journal sketches of the boy.

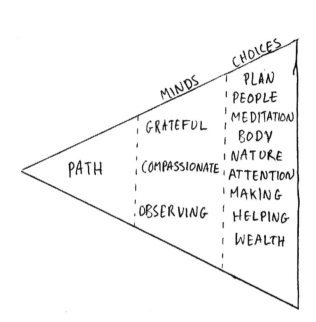

TAKE A PATH AND WALK IT WITH
A GOOD MIND AND GOOD CHOICES.

My PATH Notes

My PATH Notes

My PATH Notes

My PATH Notes

My PATH Notes

Jeuveau

S. Korea

make product better
   cheaper
manufacturer

Xeomin
   immunogenic

300 size molecular
        weight
900 kilodalton

Made in the USA
Columbia, SC
25 August 2020